Make Money Moonlighting!

The 4 Best Ways To Earn Money With Your Computer and The 4 Traps To Avoid.

By

John R. Mortz

The American Institute of Computer Technology
30 N. Raymond Ave. Suite 714
P.O. Box 2615
Pasadena, CA 91102-2615 • (818) 793-8429

First Printing August 1989

ISBN 0-9623722-2-6 Softcover

Disclaimer

The information published in this book represents the opinions, personal research, and business experience of the author. Since the success of any business enterprise depends upon the skill and ability of the person operating the business, the author makes no guarantees and disclaims any personal loss or liabilities that may occur as a result of the use of the information contain herein.

"This publication is designed to provide accurate and authoritative information in regard to the subject matter covered in it. It is provided with the understanding that the publisher is not engaged in rendering legal, accounting, or other professional services. If legal advice or other expert assistance is required, the services of a competent professional person should be sought."

From a declaration of principals jointly adopted by a committee of the American Bar Association and a committee of Publishers and Associations.

Table Of Contents

Preface ii

Chapter I
INTRODUCTION 1

Chapter 2
AREAS OF OPPORTUNITY 12

Chapter 3
THE BEST WAYS TO PROFIT 19

Chapter 4
WORD PROCESSING 31

Chapter 5
DESKTOP PUBLISHING 49

Chapter 6
SHAREWARE DEVELOPMENT 65

Chapter 7
COMPUTER CONSULTING 76

Chapter 8
FOUR TRAPS TO AVOID 113

Chapter 9
EPILOG 119

PREFACE

I have written this book to provide you with the information that you need to start your own profitable business, moonlighting with your computer.

Make Money Moonlighting is not a book to be quickly skimmed and placed on the shelf. You simply can't get the full benefit from it by reading it just once. Keep it handy and consult it often.

As the author of this book, I perceive my job is to tell you straight out what works and what doesn't. My book, consequently, contains the knowhow for you to start your own profitable business, if you are willing to work at it. It is not a compilation of get-rich-quick schemes which lead nowhere or are so complex that no one can duplicate them. It is based on my own real life experience and the experience of others whom I have helped start their own businesses. These techniques, when used as directed, will help you succeed.

The key element in this equation, nevertheless is **YOU**. If you are to be successful in your own business, you must be willing to do everything it takes to succeed. You must be willing to put in the time necessary to achieve success. It is only then, that you will be rewarded with more money and a better life.

Chapter 1
INTRODUCTION

Having your own business can be one of the most thrilling and rewarding of all experiences that life offers you. By starting your own business, you will find that you have the opportunity to earn lots of money and have plenty of time to enjoy it.

According to statistics published by the U.S. Department of Labor, there are about 15 to 20 million Americans earning extra income outside of their regular jobs. That means that nearly 20 percent of the work force is moonlighting in some way.

> *It is not known how many people use a computer in their moonlighting activities, but it's a good bet that computer users are the fastest-growing segment of moonlighters, and that they are making the best hourly wages.*

By being a moonlighter, you control what sort of work you do, when you do it, and how much you do without giving up your regular job. Nevertheless, information seems to indicate that moonlighters using computers are turning their part-time activities into full-time businesses more often and with more success than nearly all the rest.

Make Money Moonlighting! helps you overcome the problems faced by most people wanting to get into business.

Some of us procrastinate starting our own businesses and, consequently, we never reach our goals. Some of us are afraid of failure, which is certainly justifiable. Some of us feel we can't afford the time to learn how to go in business for ourselves. And some of us feel that a good job will provide all the security we will ever need.

In reality, there are many good jobs out there. But even the best job with a large corporation can offer poor security. We know that the only constant thing in life is change. Even working for a large corporation may not offer any real security. Within hours of failing to get a certain contract, a lay-off can occur. The only real security is to have our own businesses and to be our own boss.

By moonlighting with your computer, you can have the best of all possible worlds. You continue working for someone else, thereby having the cash flow to support yourself while, at the same time, you have the opportunity to earn extra money in your own business. Moonlighting is not the only way to get started in your own business: it is only one way. In my opinion, however, moonlighting offers the best potential for long-term success, while minimizing the risks and hazards inherent in starting any new enterprise.

The next 119 pages of this book are jammed full of money-making ideas. All these ideas are derived from common sense and compiled from the success stories of 73 entrepreneurs who are presently earning extra money moonlighting with their computers. Although these case studies do not appear in this text, they are documented in the companion book to the one you are presently reading, *How To Moonlight With Your Computer*. Information about obtaining your copy of *How To Moonlight With Your Computer* appears at the end of this book.

NO DARK DEEP MAGIC SECRETS

From the conversations I have had with people interested in starting their own businesses, I have the impression that people wait and wait and wait, looking for a great idea to impel them to success. Well, it isn't necessary for you to discover a great innovative idea. You can become successful the same way most people do. Take note that 88% of the people who have established a successful business enterprise have done so by copying an established idea and then executing that idea superbly.

To show you how to copy a good business idea and execute it superbly is the purpose of this book. You will learn the ideas behind the four best ways to earn money with your computer, including marketing ideas that really work. You will be able to see what it takes to succeed. You can use the ideas presented on the following pages to become one of the very successful eighty-eight percenters.

WHERE DO GOOD BUSINESS IDEAS COME FROM?

A recent article in the June 1989 edition of INC magazine, The Origins of Entrepreneurship by John Case describes how the founders of America's fastest growing companies got started.

- 43 % Got their idea while working in the same industry.

- 15% Got their idea while watching someone else doing it. They figured that they could do it better.

- 11% Saw an unfilled niche in the consumer marketplace. (Note: Be sure to read our comments about using your competition. That's how niche's are discovered.)

- 7% Did a systematic search of the available business opportunities.

- 5% Got their idea through a brainstorm that they just can't explain.

- 3% Got their idea from their hobby.

- 16% Didn't know.

INNOVATIVE IMITATION

The focus of ***Make Money Moonlighting!*** is to show you how to use your competitors to earn money faster and easier. Your competitors have already done the research; they have already made all the mistakes. By focusing your attention on them you can emulate their success and avoid their failures.

Take a lesson from Commodore Vanderbilt, who accumulated one of Americas greatest fortunes in the 19th century. He would never start an untried business venture. He would always wait until other people, the early pioneers, rushed in, spent their time, money, effort, and energy identifying the sources of profit. Of course, many of these pioneers would go broke trying to get rich. But not the Commodore.

Once the industry was established and the survivors could be identified, Vanderbilt would analyze what those industry leaders did right. He would determine what worked and what didn't. Armed with this knowledge, he would then move in and out-compete those very same people at their own game. The Commodore used his competition to get a competitive advantage.

CREATING YOUR OWN OPPORTUNITY

More than 15 years ago, a company I was working for closed its doors. One day, I had a good job, the next I was standing in line at the California Department of Employment registering for work. While there, I overheard a conversation between two young people that had a profound effect on me. One said, "If this economy doesn't turn around, I don't think I'll ever find a job. The other responded, "Yeah, nobody's hiring."

At that time, I had the feeling that these two young people wanted to exchange their time for dollars. "I'll put in my time, you pay me for it." That wasn't bad. In fact, it was what I had been doing. It's the American way. The laborer is worthy of his hire...and so forth.

I made up my mind at the Employment Office that I would change my modus operandi. I would go back to work for a large company — which I did — but I would keep my eyes open to opportunities which would assure me that I could have a business of my own!

I was more fortunate than some, perhaps. I had a good education and excellent credentials. And, through no fault of my own, I was unemployed! I vowed that I would work harder than I had ever done so that, should a similar condition show itself again, I would be prepared.

I began to take an active interest in computers. I learned how to operate them and what makes them work. At every opportunity,

I learned just one more thing about these remarkable machines, believing when the time came, I could provide a service for people just like myself who might be able to use computers to start their own businesses.

Today, I do that. I don't have a job, per se. I work some hours as a computer consultant and I enjoy the work. I can state without bragging that I am an excellent computer consultant. I am never without work today.

I spend most of my time, however, helping people get started in their own businesses. That's why I wrote this book. To share my experiences with you. So that you, too, can become your own employer, so that you can spread your wings and do whatever you want to do. And I believe you will find moonlighting with your computer will provide you with a better income, more free time, and the satisfaction of a job well done.

BE ACTIVE, NOT PASSIVE

Everyone who started a small home-based business and watched it grow into a major enterprise, listened to the voice of action. This manual is written to help you get started and establish momentum. It is written to help you make something happen. It is written to help you find a need and fill it. It is written to show you how to moonlight with your computer. When you are ready, tell the world that you are here. Tell people how they will benefit by doing business with you. This manual will show you how. If you follow its precepts and directions, you will never worry again about finding a job.

In the beginning, you will have to work hard and think smart. There will be times you must pass up fishing trips or a night at the theater to finish a project for a desperate client. There will be times when you need to take the money you saved for your vacation and buy some much needed equipment. You may wonder why you are doing it, but the end result will make it all worthwhile.

MAKE SOMETHING HAPPEN

I can remember just a few years ago when people talked about earning extra money in their spare time. Now, I don't know anyone who has any spare time. Every minute of every hour of every day is booked up. Even if it's just watching TV, or going shopping, or attending a ball game, people use every second of their waking hours to perform some activity. In fact, the average American spends over 7 hours every day just watching TV.

If you want to succeed as a moonlighter, you must be willing to do everything it takes to succeed. If that means giving up Dallas to J.R. and Sue Ellen, so be it. If you want to take charge of your life . . . and make something happen, it could open the door to a very exciting and profitable life. You must organize your time and stick to your priorities. And you must start right now preparing to be a success. I can teach you how to moonlight with your computer, but the dedication and desire to succeed must come from within YOU!

MOONLIGHTING MADE SIMPLE

The hardest part of getting started is—getting started. Most of us think about it, discuss it, plan it, and dream about it.

If you want to have your own business, start it NOW! You never know what ideas will work until you give them a chance.

How many times have you had an idea, only to read in the paper or hear on television about someone else who beat you to it and turned your idea into a success story?

DON'T WAIT

That happened to me, too. In the 1970's when I started my first business, I wanted to form a corporation, but I didn't have the money to pay an attorney to do the work. So, I went to the law library for a couple of days and researched what I would need to do. I prepared the Articles of Incorporation and took them to the California Secretary of State's office. Lo and behold, the examiner passed them. I was a corporation.

Friends thought it was marvelous. I had my own corporation, and I did it without an attorney. "Write a book," they told me. "Tell other people how to do it." "Good idea," I said. "'I'll do it just as soon as I tie up these loose ends." Well, there are several books on the market right now on this very same subject. The first book appeared two years after I had incorporated. Unfortunately, I wasn't the author. I had not gotten around to writing it. It became a best seller and made the author a bundle of money. I still see it advertised today. But that is just another story about a fish that got away.

I did learn one important thing from that experience, though: whenever I get an idea I put it to the test right away. No more procrastination for me. Don't make the same mistake that I did. Get started with your money-making ideas, RIGHT NOW!

Study your strongest idea and start researching and testing it. Begin by reading up on it and talking to people in the field. Tell other people about your idea and get their reactions. Whenever you get a negative reaction from anyone, analyze why. Is there a valid reason behind that reaction? You may have gotten such a response simply because someone was jealous of your ambition. If the idea still seems good, develop a step-by-step plan to test it. Put your idea into action.

KEEP YOUR JOB

If you have a job, keep it. Establish a business plan to get started. Include a budget to cover your expenses until your business is going. Incorporate into that plan one of the approaches to get started in your own business. They are:

1. <u>Moonlighting</u>
   Keep your full-time job and develop your business as a sideline. When it starts to grow, you can quit your job and run it full time, if you like. You need to make a firm commitment to work at least eight hours a week in your own business to make it viable.

2. <u>Working Part Time</u>
   Work a part-time job to provide a base income while you're building up the business. When the business income covers your basic expenses, drop the part-time job.

3. <u>Spinning-off</u>
   Turn your previous employer into your first major customer or, when ethically possible, take a major client with you from your previous job.

4. <u>Financial Cushion</u>
   Find a financial resource to support yourself while you develop your business. Your cushion should be large enough to cover basic expenses for at least eight months.

You can use any of these approaches when you start your own business. Of course I favor moonlighting and recommend that you consider it as your avenue to success.

WHAT YOU SHOULD DO NEXT

In order to manage the requirements of your current job along with the demands of your new moonlighting business, you will need to do some thinking about phasing your new activities into your daily schedule.

Remember, the primary advantage of moonlighting is that you keep your present job until your moonlighting business grows large enough to allow you to quit your job and concentrate on your moonlighting, full time. Consequently, you don't want to do any thing that will jeopardize your job. In the beginning your job is your most important asset. So, plan on keeping it for a while. Moonlighting is not a get rich quick scheme, but a planned program for starting your own business.

EASING INTO IT

If you have been employed on the same job for any length of time, you have probably established a known pattern of behavior around the office. Your coworkers have become accustomed to it and know what to expect from you. If you start spending a lot of time on the telephone with one of your moonlighting clients, people will notice. Your boss will notice, too. So we advise against conducting your moonlighting business at your regular job.

If you normally play cards with the gang during your lunch hour and then you suddenly start taking two hour lunches to promote your moonlighting activities, people will notice, and start talking or even complaining. If you want to keep your job, maintain a low profile for your outside activities.

Install an answering machine and make arrangements to talk to your clients in the evenings or early in the morning. If you are expected to play cards everyday at lunch, start missing one day a week to "go for a walk" or "work on your income taxes". It won't take long for your coworkers to adjust to your new behavior pattern, so it won't surprise them when you start taking two days a week off from the game. In two or three months, your lunch hours will become yours to use for your own business and no one will wonder what you are doing.

FREEDOM FROM OVERHEAD

When you start your moonlighting business from home you do not have any rent to pay or payroll to worry about. When you earn some money, be very careful about spending it. Do not add any equipment or overhead unless you are certain it will help you make money faster. If it doesn't, try to get along without it for a while longer.

Think twice before hiring an assistant or a bookkeeper. Put in the extra time. Work a little harder. Do the boring, tedious tasks yourself. Accumulate capital. Saving money for future expansion is more important than increasing efficiency or employing the latest technology. Adding equipment or hiring people too soon can lead to financial disaster. Some moonlighters avoid increasing their overhead by operating from home and never moving out to an office.

Chapter 2
AREAS OF OPPORTUNITY

When you start your business, there are just two things that you can do: You can offer a service, or you can manufacture a product. You must decide which of these two things you want to do. Nevertheless, in deciding whether you will offer a service or manufacture a product, there are primary advantages to both that you will want to consider.

Of these two areas, the service sector is the fastest growing segment of the economy. People are willing to pay high prices for convenience. The ability to save time is worth money to your clients. The major advantage of starting a service-oriented business, consequently, is that you can establish cash flow quickly. By utilizing the methods outlined in the text, even beginners can find their first client in the matter of days.

Take the case of Laura who provides administrative consulting services to attorneys. She automates the paperwork for dozens of attorneys. She understands the requirements of her customers. Computer vendors respect her ability to negotiate the best price. Attorneys like her because she gets the jobs done quickly and within budget. Over the years she has built up an extensive network of contacts. These people know her and like her work. She can always get work from any of her former employers doing word processing or providing paralegal services. When she leaves her last job on a Friday, she has two more jobs lined up by 8 a.m. the next Monday.

The example of Laura shows how persistent and consistent your income can be by offering services. You can earn top wages in the service sector. However, the major disadvantage of the service businesses is that you can't get rich offering services. No matter how much you charge, you can work just so many hours a day. This places an eventual cap on your earnings.

Products, on the other hand, offer the greatest growth potential. By developing software or publishing information, you do the job just one time. But you can then sell an unlimited number of copies of that item. Whenever someone anywhere in the world buys it, you make money. Unfortunately, it can take one to two years to develop and market a product. If you need cash, right now, manufacturing products is not for you.

OPPORTUNITIES IN PRODUCTS

The opportunities in products are found in publishing, software, hardware, retail trade, and miscellaneous. I will elaborate on each of them and indicate which ones will offer you the greatest potential for future success.

PUBLISHING

This category, which includes desktop publishing, offers some of the most outstanding opportunities to the home office entrepreneur to succeed in a big way. The two best ways to do this are: first, to self-publish books and manuals; second, to publish a newsletter. There are not many products that allow you to resell an item at 10 to 20 times what it costs you to produce.

Other products you can produce are: magazine articles, special reports, classified directories and newspapers, guidebooks, cookbooks, software tutorials, and instruction manuals for other software developers.

SOFTWARE

There are always opportunities in software. Every time a new hardware system is developed, new software must be created. Software that ran on the old hardware needs to be converted to run on the new hardware.

If you opt for this avenue, remember that there is a long lead time to develop good software. Be prepared to spend one to two years working on the project. When you finally get it to market, you may be faced with software pirates. Piracy can cut your sales and revenues in half. Unfortunately, that is part of the game.

Another area of opportunity here that may be less risky is to develop shareware programs. It may be the best way to get started as a software developer. Shareware is a method to let the customer try it before he buys it. Once you have completed development of your software product, all you have to do is to distribute copies to user's groups, remote bulletin board systems, and shareware distributors. People will then get copies of it for free. If they like it, they are asked to register it with you for a nominal fee. You make your money by offering manuals and updates to the registered owners.

Other forms of software include video tapes and audio cassettes. People are producing these products for the training market to explain new products.

HARDWARE

The best opportunities in hardware lie in manufacturing peripherals, accessories, keyboard templates, and computer furniture. There is just too much competition to hope to earn much money producing computer systems. Many clones are sold at cost just to get the add-on sales of software and peripherals. Development of logic boards and adapters can be profitable, but it takes a lot of specialized knowledge. If you do not have an established distribution channel to market your product, you may face some tough sledding.

RETAIL TRADE

Retail trade includes selling hardware, peripherals, accessories, supplies, software products, and books. Promoting swap meets or brokering used equipment can be classified as a retail activity. Renting computers or desktop publishing equipment also falls into this classification. In fact, if you sell computer-related merchandise by direct mail, you should consider yourself a retailer.

Computer repair is retail trade since you sell services to the public. Direct sales through computer-assisted telemarketing or multilevel marketing plans can also be profitable activities.

MISCELLANEOUS

Other products that you can produce for sale to the public include T-shirts, calendars, biorhythm charts, crossword puzzles, banners, and video portraits. Genealogical research projects producing family trees can be profitable, too. Perhaps one of the best opportunities in this category would be the creation of a computer game or puzzle for the home entertainment market. If it catches on, it can be a big winner.

OPPORTUNITIES IN SERVICES

There are many more opportunities in services than in products. People are thinking of new ways all the time to apply a computer to earning money in the service sector of the economy. Today, however, the opportunities can be broken down into five distinct areas. They are consulting, training, data base, service brokering, and word processing related services.

CONSULTING

Computer consulting is, perhaps, the premier, high-prestige opportunity available to the home entrepreneur. You can earn top money performing needs assessments and system installation for small businesses. You can specialize in programming, networking, engineering, CAD/CAM, and/or any other field that interests you.

TRAINING

Education and training is a wide open field. You can earn money as a private tutor or sponsor seminars and workshops. People need to learn how to operate their hardware. Then they need help learning the features of their software. The constant barrage of new programs leaves the public with inadequate knowledge of what programs to use. New word processors, spreadsheets, and integrated programs are flooding the market.

This means opportunity for you to offer training to both adults and children.

DATA BASE RELATED ACTIVITIES.

The ability for computers to store large amounts of data and retrieve it quickly is the true driving force behind all computer applications and needs. This is most plainly evident in data base applications. Public data bases such as the Source, Compuserve, and Dialog have fostered opportunities for information brokers to sell data base research to their clients. The technology to allow personal computers to store 20, 40, 60, 100 megabytes and more information on a hard disk has led to the development of remote bulletin board systems.

Sports handicapping is a data base application. Economic forecasting is data base related. Stock market investment and commodity speculation revolve around huge data bases. Electronic mail, baby sitting services, computer dating all require data bases. Accounting and bookkeeping systems are data base applications. There are plenty of opportunities in data base applications. Unless you have good business skills, data base may be lower profit activities than some of the other alternatives that you will be able to choose from.

SERVICE BROKERAGE

Brokering temporary help may be one of the growth industries of the future. Although data base application programs are used to manage the paperwork, this is a people business. You must recruit people into your talent pool, and then you must find employers who want their services. If you like people, you can become very successful brokering word processors, consultants, trainers, and programmers.

Even managers and supervisors are hired on temporary bases. One such service I heard of was called "Rent-A-Boss." It provided supervisory personnel while the boss was on vacation or when a larger company needed a temporary department head until a permanent employee could be found.

WORD PROCESSING RELATED SERVICES

By far, word processing related services offers the novice the best chance of operating his or her own business from home. You can start as a straight word processor or you can combine the tools of word processing with other skills.

Public relations firms must produce press releases. A word processor lets them customize the releases to each recipient. Specialized business reports such as SBA financial packaging is a word processing application. So is the preparation of legal documents such as incorporation papers. The same is true of medical transcriptions. Bill collecting requires the use of a series of form letters.

You can personalize each one with your word processor. The import/export industry requires repetitive paperwork. Proposal writing, resumes, business plan writing, book reviews, restaurant menus, environmental impact reports, student dissertations are all documents that have the same format each time it is prepared. These are natural word processing related applications.

Chapter 3
THE BEST WAYS TO PROFIT

There are lots of ways of using a computer to produce goods and services that other people want and are willing to pay good money to receive. We know of 102 ways and people are thinking of new ways all the time. However, some of the ways offer better long term earning prospects than some of the others. Those ways have proven themselves in the marketplace. Cost effective methods of promoting these businesses are well established. Learning about the four best ways to earn money with your computer may also help give you other good related money-making ideas.

THE MOST DIFFICULT PART

Remember that it's not necessary for you to discover the perfect way to moonlight. Ideas evolve and change with time. You will get many more ideas once you plunge into the fray. Don't wait to complete a course of study or gain some academic credentials before getting started. Your potential clients are interested in practical know-how that is developed only through on the job experience. Most likely your first assignment will be very different from what you have dreamed of. Take it anyway. You will gain experience and be earning money while you are learning.

PROVEN MARKETS

By the time you finish this chapter you will have been introduced to the four best ways of earning money with your computer. These four ways are the products of intensive research. They have demonstrated their long-term earnings potential and they have proven markets. Think back to Chapter 1. On page three I pointed out to you that 88% of all people who are successful in their own business have achieved their success by taking a known idea and executing it superbly. They have learned from Commodore Vanderbilt to let their competiors invest time, money and effort into proving the economic potential of an industry. Then they have utilized what works and discarded what doesn't to obtain a competitive advantage.

The ideas that you will receive from *Make Money Moonlighting* offer you the best potential for success because other people are actually out there doing it. You are going to discover the marketing ideas that these successful moonlighters use to attract customers and clients. When you finish reading this material, you will have enough knowledge to set out on your own.

COMPETITION IS GOOD

This key point—that competition is good—will be repeated so often that you will no doubt be sick of hearing it by the end of this book. But I repeat it in different ways because it is so difficult for most people to accept. Most people are concerned if competition exists. They feel that if there is competition, it is too late to get started. The absolute opposite is true. The presence of competition enhances your likelihood of having a successful moonlighting venture.

You should thank your competition. They validity of your moonlighting ideas in the m being there first, they have developed techniqu strategies for communicating the existence of the products and services to their customers. Your successful competitors know what works and what doesn't. Whenever a new product or a new business idea is introduced into the market, potential customers must be educated about that new idea and taught why a given product or service will benefit them. Your competitors blazed new trails, introduced new products, and spent their time, money, and effort educating customers.

Gathering information about potential competition is one of the most important aspects of getting started in your own business. Not only will you learn what the traps and pitfalls are, and how to avoid them, you may discover a gold mine in an unfilled niche waiting for you to take advantage of it. Once you have decided on what you will pursue, you should begin assessing your competitors. A convenient checklist for you to use to do that is presented later in this chapter.

Remember, even though IBM dominates the computer business, Apple still makes plenty of money. Even though the big three television networks dominate the airwaves, HBO, CNN, and even Home Shoppers have carved out profitable niches on cable.

HOW TO COLLECT INFORMATION

Start collecting information on people who are already doing the kinds of things that you would like to do. Find out how many people are doing it, how much they charge, where they do it, what they will be doing next, and anything else you can uncover. Buy their books, subscribe to their publications, attend their seminars. The trick to collecting this type of information is not to let your competitor know that you are thinking of starting your own business. Obviously, no one is going to tell their success secrets to a potential competitor.

Pilgrim's Progress—How One Consultant Learned the Hard Way.

One of my friends decided to become a software consultant. He had great credentials from years of programming and systems analysis experience with major corporations. He had a general idea that personal contact was the way to develop his business, but all he did was hand out business cards. He tried advertising. The phone rang only once; it was a life insurance salesman. In desperation, he called a successful software consultant whom he knew, and told him that he was now a software consultant and would like some tips on the most effective ways to market his services.

Not surprisingly, the only advice he received was, "Hand out your business cards to everyone you meet and advertise in the yellow pages." We know how far doing those things had got him so far. My friend tried another consultant who told him, "Write technical articles. People will read them and call you." That was actually good advice, but it didn't assist my friend because it contained only part of the information he needed. The problem with the advice was that my friend didn't know how to deal with editors or what to write about, so he was never able to use the idea to any advantage.

He went back to the first consultant and complained that the marketing strategy he was given wasn't working. The advice he got? "Keep trying. Eventually people will hear about you and call you." Fortunately for my friend, he did find out, before it was too late, why their marketing advice was incomplete and ineffective.

By calling local consultants and asking for help in marketing his services, he was perceived, rightly, as potential competition. Who in their right mind would actually give help to a competitor? What he did finally, to find someone who would tell him what he needed to know, was to go out-of-state. Once he was not a direct competitor anymore, other consultants would share war stories with him. They told him what he needed to know to use personal presentation methods. He found out that selling a service requires allowing your clients to meet you and decide that they like you. Personal presentation and word-of-mouth promotion is the only cost effective way that a high-priced service such as consulting can be promoted.

THE MOST IMPORTANT THING YOU CAN DO

Gathering information about the competition is one of the most important things to do to prepare for starting your own business. At the very least you learn what the traps and pitfalls are and how to avoid them. You may even discover a gold mine in an unfilled niche waiting for you to take advantage of it. You need to do a very complete survey of the consulting field. Use the Competitor's Checklist form on the following pages and fill one out for as many competitors as seems useful. Photocopy as many copies of the checklist as you need. (As long as you are using this form to promote your own business, you have my permission to copy it as often as you like.) Start a "Competitors" file for them in case you need to refer to them for ideas and information.

Competitor's Checklist

1. Name of Competitor: ____________________
   Address ____________________
   ____
   ____
   Telephone ____________________

2. Services Offered: ____________________
   ____
   ____
   ____
   ____
   ____

3. Where Does He Perform Them?
   ____
   ____
   ____

4. How Much Does He Charge? ____________________
   ____
   ____

5. Does He Have a Brochure or Portfolio?
Describe : ______________________________

____

____

6. What Promotional Materials (Articles, etc.)
Does He Have: __________________________

____

____

7. What Promotional Methods Does He Use
To Attract New Business?

____

____

____

8. What Do People Think of Him ?

____

____

____

9. What Seminars Has He Appeared at?
Conducted?

____

____

10. Referrals Available from His Clients.
Yes _____ ? No ________?
What Did They Like? What Needed Improvement? Other?
No. 1 Comments:

____

____

____

No.2 Comments:

____

____

____

No.3 Comments:

____

____

____

11. What Will He Be Doing Next ?

____

____

____

12. What Books and/or Articles Has He Written or Have Been Written About Him?

____

____

ELEVEN OF THE MOST PROFITABLE WAYS TO EARN MONEY IN THE 1990'S

From intensive research into the success secrets of entrepreneurs and individuals who are presently earning money with their computers, I have identified the eleven best ways to earn money with your computer. They are:

- Word Processing
- Desktop Publishing
- Shareware Development
- Computer Consulting
- Computer Training
- Computer Repair
- Computer Services Broker
- Computer Seminars
- Bulletin Board System
- Computer Equipment Rentals
- Employment Agency

Word processing, Desktop Publishing, Shareware Development, and Computer Consulting are discussed in this work. In my opinion they are the four best ways of earning money that I know of. The other ways that are mentioned above, including 73 brief case studies, are discussed in the advanced text, *How To Moonlight With Your Computer*.

WAYS THAT SEEM ATTRACTIVE, BUT AREN'T

There are many, many ways of earning money with your computer. It is possible to earn money with all of them.

However, my research has shown that there are certain ways that should be avoided for one reason or another. They are really traps or pitfalls for the unwary. Conditions may change and these ways may become neglected opportunities that will offer some enterprising individual a chance to jump in and make a lot of money. Until that happens, I will not be able to recommend them to you. For the time being, I will just list them. In Chapter Eight I will go into all the reasons why I feel they do not offer you the best economic potential. These ways are:

- Accounting Services
- Tax Preparation Services
- Information Broker
- Software Locator

SKILLS YOU WILL NEED

Each business idea needs a different degree of business and technical skill for that business to be operated successfully.

The point I want to make is that different opportunities require different skills to become a success. In order to operate your own business, you must have BOTH technical and business knowledge. The more complex the business, the more specialized is the knowledge you need. Word processing requires the least amount of technical skills and a modest amount of business skills. For most people, it is the logical place to begin.

As time goes on you can develop your skills and move into other areas that offer you better potential. The unveiling of unexpected opportunities as you progress towards your business goals is one of the nicest things that ever happens to you. For that one reason alone, it is worthwhile for you to stop what you are doing and get started, today.

DIFFERENT LEVELS OF KNOWLEDGE

Each of the four ways mentioned previously require different levels of technical and business ability. Word processing needs the least technical and business skill. Many word processing programs have become so simple to operate all you need to do is simply switch on your computer. Spelling-checkers and even style-checkers have reduced grammatical knowledge to a minimum. Business skills are basic. You can get started with enough accounting skill to keep track of income and expenses and the savvy to estimate the cost of a job .

Desktop publishing, on the other hand, is more complex. The computer skills for layout text and graphics on a page can be learned in a week or two. The business skills are different. If you operate as a design shop for brochures, producing newsletters for others, and graphics design, they are not any more complex than those required for operating a word processing business. However, if you enter the high profit arena of publishing your own books and/or newsletters, considerable knowledge is required. In fact a discussion of what is required to be a successful publisher is beyond the scope of this book. If you are intrigued by desktop publishing, think of starting as a "Second Generation" word processor.

Shareware development is an area which requires high technical skill. Advanced programming and computer knowledge are required just to develop the software. But the business skills are not as complex as those required for success as a commercial software developer. You use FREE distribution channels to entice users to try your program before they buy it. You make your money by getting your users to register their free copy with you and then you sell them the updates and improved versions of the product.

Computer consulting is the most prestigious of all the ways that we know about. However, it requires both a high degree of technical skill and a high degree of business skill to be successful in this area. It is not an area for everybody. I do not recommend that most people try to begin their moonlighting careers as a computer consultant. It is very difficult. Yet it is not the technical skill of the aspiring consultant that is my concern. It is the subtle business skills that need to be nurtured and developed by everyone who wants to consult. First on my list is the ability to listen for your clients needs and the ability to communicate to your client that you have solved similar problems before.

Chapter 4
WORD PROCESSING

Word processing is one of the most popular and easiest ways of earning money with your computer. In fact, it may be the very best way for you to begin. If you have never had your own business, this is especially true. The duties of a person who does word processing are well documented and understood. It is easy for you to focus on your target market. It is simple to use your competitors to find a niche. It gives you time to develop a problem-solving attitude. It gives you a chance to earn money while you are learning.

THE MOST VERSATILE OF ALL COMPUTER-RELATED OPPORTUNITIES

Before delving deeper into the details of starting and operating a word processing business, let's stop for a few minutes and examine precisely what you can do:

- operate a general typing service
- type books, manuscripts, and screenplays
- transcribe medical and legal information
- maintain mailing lists and produce mailing labels
- provide letter writing service
- prepare business reports
- prepare resumes
- produce newsletters for others

- provide technical and scientific word processing service
- provide foreign language word processing

SKILLS YOU WILL NEED

In order to provide any of the preceding services, you will need certain skills. They are:

- the ability to type;
- the ability to operate the software;
- knowledge of grammar and punctuation;
- the ability to use word-of-mouth techniques to promote your business;
- the ability to estimate a job fairly accurately.

If you need help operating the software, there are training classes offered by community colleges and adult schools, software venders, and private trainers. By using the great word processing and spelling-checker programs that are now available, anyone can be a good secretary. All you need is a computer and a letter-quality printer. Before the development of personal computer technology, operating a typing or secretarial service required the development of typing and grammatical skills to be successful. Now with all the personal computer software available to help you, all you need to do is to be able to operate the software. If you can't type, there are computer programs available that will teach you how and tutor you to increase your speed and accuracy. If you can't spell, spelling-checkers will review every word you input. If your grammatical skills are not up to speed, style-checkers will review sentence structure and recommend improvements.

Technology has eliminated most of the technicalities of this business. You just have to be able to keyboard and to sell yourself to your clients. By following the directions and recommendations in this text, anyone can accomplish these requirements.

THE SOFTWARE

There are hundreds of word processing programs available. However, there are certain features you should consider necessary in any word processing program you select.

1. Mail merge. Mail merge capability is necessary for producing personalized mailings easily and quickly. The ability to insert field A from a data file into the proper slot in a Master Letter is mandatory if you do mass mailings for any of your clients.

2. Style sheets. A style sheet will save you a lot of time formatting and/or reformatting a client's document. By setting up a style sheet, you can change fonts, margins, tabs, spacing, etc. throughout the entire document or just in certain portions of the document with one command. Every time your client changes his or her mind about the format of a report, proposal, or letter, you can make those changes in a matter of seconds.

3. Macros. This feature is valuable when you have repetitious amounts of copy that you need to copy regularly. You create macros by recording the keystrokes as you type. After the keystrokes have been recorded, they can be repeated with one command. You save time by inserting this standardized test with a single command.

4. Sorting. Rearranging information from tables or lists takes a lot of time. A sort option lets you manipulate blocks of text and items in a table and rearrange them in the proper order.

5. Spelling-checker. This feature will help you catch spelling and typographical errors. It's absolutely indispensable.

Style-Checkers. Style-checkers designed to correct grammar are becoming more powerful and useful every day. They will analyze style, pointing out overlong sentences and passive voice constructions. They will also analyze the readability of the material, based on word length. Some new releases of this software will alert you to incomplete sentences or verb-subject agreement problems. This software can also tell the differences between homonyms, such as "its" and "it's" (contraction for *it is*).

THE POTENTIAL IN WORD PROCESSING

The potential market for this service is vast. Small businesses are springing up everywhere. Many of these small companies will be eager to use your services. It is far more economical to use a word-processing or secretarial service than it is to hire someone full-time. This is especially true if the company does not already own a computer.

BECOME A TEMPORARY OVERLOAD SERVICE BUREAU

Keep your eyes open and you will see temporary, overload word processing services springing up in the most unexpected places. For example, I was recently having lunch with a friend who has an office in a high-rise office complex in the nicest business district of Los Angeles. Getting off the elevator on the fourteenth floor, I noticed a large, handwritten sign that was taped to an office door near his. It read, "Booked-Up Until Friday." This was noon on Wednesday. What could that sign mean? The only other sign on the door was the suite number.

Being curious about it, I walked in and introduced myself. It turned out that this business was a word processing service specializing in legal documents. Two women performed word processing services for attorneys on an overload basis only. Since most lawyers have their own word processors, you wouldn't realize, offhand, how powerful the demand for this service might be. Whenever a crisis hits, however, the lawyers in that building farm out the overload to the women on the fourteenth floor.

When the women have plenty of work, they place a sign on the door and accept no more work that week. And when they run out of work, what do they do? These women are smart. They have formed a network of contacts with every law office in the building. All they have to do is telephone or visit their friends in the building until they find someone who is overloaded and needs assistance during this emergency. They don't have to sell anything. They just offer a service to help solve someone else's problem. It's really quite simple when you know how.

SOURCES OF POTENTIAL CUSTOMERS

Finding clients is easy if you use the concept discussed previously. The average office has a crisis or emergency at least once a week. Build your business by becoming a personalized service for overload work. Provide a service that solves someone else's problems. It can make you very successful. The more problems you solve for other people, the more money you'll make. Produce results for them and they will tell their friends. Your business will flourish. All you have to do is to develop a problem-solving attitude.

There is a nearly inexhaustible number of potential clients for your word processing service. The following are just a few of the places or groups of people who have a need for your services.

- Small businesses — General office work.
- Students —Term papers, theses, dissertations,etc.
- Writers — Manuscripts, transcriptions, notes, outlines, etc.
- Academic field — For professors and researchers: research reports, grant proposals, manuscripts.
- Legal profession — Briefs, transcriptions, wills, contracts, etc.
- Court reporters — Transcriptions.
- General public — Flyers, resumes, Christmas letters, etc.
- Medical profession — Insurance claims, billings, case histories, transcriptions, manuals.
- Real estate companies, agents — Mailings to prospects, letters, flyers, promotions.
- Associations — Newsletters, correspondence, mailings, etc.
- Restaurants — Menus.
- Printers — Price lists, advertising flyers.
- Engineers — Specifications, tables, charts, proposals, letters.
- Home office workers — Not all of these people have a computer; they may need general office help.
- Public Relations — Press releases, advertising copy, brochures.

- Consultants — Proposals, presentations, reports, contracts.
- Contractors — Proposals, invoices, schedules, letters.
- Architects — Reports, specifications, proposals
- Wholesalers — Letters of inquiry, contracts, proposals, etc.
- Furniture dealers — Mailings to customers, letters, invoices.

One of the excuses that I hear all the time from people who want to start earning money with their computers is that they don't know where they will get customers. Just those preceding twenty ideas could keep you very busy. And that's just the beginning. How many other places can you think of? There are plenty of people out there who need your help. But you must:

- get out and meet them;
- make them your friends;
- ask for the order.

Don't be afraid to just go out there and ask. Remember, you're providing a service that many people want and need.

WAYS TO GET EXPERIENCE IF YOU NEED IT

If you do not have any experience in general office work, or if you want to get started in another area where your experience is severely limited, go to work for a temporary agency. The agency will send you out on many diverse assignments. If you have never worked in an office before, you will have an opportunity to learn what would be required of you when you are out on your own. Perhaps you have experience with engineering specifications, but want to work in public relations. A temporary agency can place you with an advertising firm that specializes in producing press releases and product brochures.

In this way, you can gain experience that will be invaluable when you are ready to go out on your own. Another thing to keep in mind about registering with a temporary agency is that the demand for word processing personnel is so great that many agencies offer FREE training courses.

PRICING YOUR SERVICE

Even before you get your first client, you will be asked "How much do you charge?" You must be prepared to answer professionally without hesitation. But in order to answer this question you must be aware of all the variables that go into establishing your price.

HIDDEN COSTS

When you are prospecting for new clients, who pays for your time? And when you are delivering a manuscript all the way across town to meet a printing deadline, who pays for your driving time and car expenses? When you are preparing a transcription and one of your clients calls to chat, who pays for that? And when a client leaves town for a two-week vacation and asks you to drop by his office and collect his mail, who pays for that?

The answer to that is very obvious: The client pays for everything. If you do not charge him for special services, then you will pay. Perhaps you will not spend any money, yet you will lose your time and forego the opportunity of increasing your income. You must keep a careful log of the time spent working for every client and bill accordingly.

HOW TO SET YOUR PRICE

First of all, you must decide how much money you need to earn. It is the amount of money that you will pay yourself for performing word processing services. Be careful, now, it's not the same as the amount of money that you charge your clients. What you charge your clients is your billing rate. It will be the sum of your hourly rate plus overhead plus fringe benefits plus profit.

Second, you must take into consideration the cost of your computer, software, printer, and other equipment. That equipment must be amortized and its cost must be recovered from your business income. Add this onto your hourly rate.

Third, you must consider operating costs such as the cost of paper and supplies, the cost of disks and ribbons, and the cost of getting your equipment repaired whenever it breaks down. You must determine how many business calls you make and how much they cost. Add this amount on, too.

Fourth, you must consider how much your office space costs. If you work at home, you will not have to pay rent. By not incurring this expense, you can keep your overhead costs down and not have to pass them on to your clients. Moonlighting at home with your computer will give you a cost advantage over your competitors.

Fifth, you must determine how much money you are going to spend on advertising, promotion, and publicity. Although publicity is free and will not cause you any cash outlay, there is a cost associated with it. That cost is your time, and you must be paid for that time, too.

Finally, you must be compensated for the costs of unworked time—travel, marketing, freebies, and so forth. As we noted earlier, the client pays for everything. Any fringe benefits such as sick time, health insurance, or vacation that you might expect to obtain from your work should be included here.

CHARGING BY THE PAGE

For most jobs, you will charge by the page. Once you've determined what your hourly rate should be, you can determine your per page charge very easily. Simply divide your hourly rate by the average number of pages you can type per hours and that's it.

For example, if you have set your hourly charge at $35 per hour and you can type six (6) pages an hour (of single spaced, unformatted text), your per page charge would be:

$$\$35.00/\text{hour} \div 6\ \text{pages/hour} = \$5.83/\text{page}$$

It doesn't look professional to charge an odd number of cents per page, so you would round that number up to $6.00 per page for most of your clients. For other clients who give you a lot of repeat business and for whom your marketing expenses are, therefore, less, you could charge $5.00 per page.

PRICE SHOPPERS

You will meet many price shoppers as you do more and more marketing. Be prepared for them. Whenever you meet a client who starts questioning your price, the best policy is to let them go to someone else. Your time is better spent finding clients who like you, trust your ability to get the job done, know you are being fair with them, and feel that you are worth your price.

TELEPHONE QUOTATIONS

Sometimes you will be called on the telephone for a price quotation. It is not good business, however, to quote any job without seeing it first. So what do you do? Tell the caller that you would like to see the job first and then reassure the person that you are competitive with temporary agencies and other word processors. Quote your per page rate if the caller insists on a price. Do not quote your billing rate. Your per page rate is a lower figure than your billing rate and is therefore psychologically better for attracting new business.

SELLING YOUR WORD PROCESSING SERVICES

People will buy your services only if they like you. People don't buy anything from anyone they don't like, no matter how cheap it may be or how badly they need it.

STEPS FOR SELLING YOUR SERVICE

The fastest way to get started selling your word processing services is to visit each of your prospective clients and offer your services face-to-face. Just a short visit is all that is necessary.

The following are suggestions on how to proceed. They coach you on what you will and will not need to do and tell you how to approach companies and organizations. The suggested procedure is a step-by-step plan that is easy to follow and always creates results.

WHAT YOU WILL NEED

The list of what you will and won't need to get business as a word processor may surprise you. You actually need very little to get going.

√ Business Cards: The Most Important Item.

Have business cards made up. Make them look professional; nothing fancy or cute. Your card should list just your name, the name of your business if you have one, and your telephone number.

Don't put a picture of yourself on it. Pictures are not necessary on a business card because you already talking to your prospect and have their attention. The important information is your phone number. Make sure you use large enough type so people see it immediately and can call you.

As soon as you have your cards made up, start handing them out. When you hand out your card, be sure to give two cards and say, "Here's one for a friend." There are lots of times people are asked for referrals and would give out your card, but they can't because they have already given you card to someone else. By giving out two cards in the beginning, you double your chances of getting referrals with very little expenditure of money.

WHAT YOU WON'T NEED

Don't bother to make up flyers or advertisements. Don't make up stationery yet. You'll save money if you wait until you start getting good cash flow before having stationery printed. Based on the experience of successful word processors, we feel that doing things of this nature won't yield enough business to pay for doing them.

MAKING CONTACTS

The steps in making contacts are quite simple and there really are only four steps. Remember that you are making contacts, not selling, so don't get nervous about these steps.

√ <u>Compile a list of 25 companies that can use your service.</u>

Do not put large corporations on your list first. Find smaller companies in a line of work that you are familiar with; they will be your best prospects. Some knowledge of the workings of a company will help you to approach the companies with more confidence, which in turn will inspire confidence in those you approach.

√ <u>Find out who is in charge, the decision maker.</u>

You must find out who will be making the decisions about contracting your services. This will save you a lot of time and aggravation. Call ahead to get the names of the people you want to see.

√ Make personal visits to each of those 25 companies.

Go to the first company and ask to speak to the decision maker. If the decision maker is not available, talk to his or her assistant. If the assistant is not available, talk to anyone. Your message is short, so people won't mind talking to you. You will need to cultivate all of these people anyway. Remember, your goals here are to contact the companies and to give the people there a chance to get to like you.

√ Tell them about you and your services. Don't try to "sell" them.

Offer your services by saying something along the following lines, but in your own words.

"Hi, I'm (your name) and I have a word processing business located nearby. I was in the area and thought I would stop by and say Hi. If you ever find you have a work overload or need temporary help because someone is out sick, I'm available to help you. Here's my card. Call me when you need some assistance. Thanks for your time."

You want to give a short, sweet, polite presentation, then leave TWO business cards.

√ Then go to the next company, and the next, until you have visited all 25 companies.

Remember, you're not trying to sell your service, you're just telling the people at each of the 25 companies about them. You have to give them a chance to see if they like you.

√ After you have visited those 25 companies, STOP.

Do not keep visiting 25 new companies. You are already known to your 25 companies and they are now your very best prospects. Don't expect to get work right away. Rarely will one of those companies hire you on the first visit. You're selling a service, and to sell a service, your clients need to know you first. The next major step is to go back. That is when you will start generating business.

FOLLOWING UP: THE NEXT STEP

Follow-up is the key to getting clients, the secret of success. By following up you are setting yourself apart from everyone else. Very few people ever follow up. By doing so, you will show yourself to be someone that they want working for them. It shows that you are someone who sticks to things and puts your money where your mouth is.

√ Go back to each of the companies right away—within a few days.

Make it a point to start your rounds to your companies again as soon as you can. You want the persons you met to remember who you are. You'll know best by that time how to present yourself to the person you met at each company, but you'll want to say something like:

"Hi. Remember me, I was in a few days ago. I can do all word processing jobs, large and small and I'm available to help you whenever you're in a crunch or are short-staffed or just want some help to catch up."

Then give them TWO MORE business cards. And again, thank them for their time. They are busy people with a lot to do, and will appreciate your politeness.

It would be surprising if you have to go back to all 25 companies before you get your first client. By the time you drop in the second time, somebody will be having a crisis and will need you to help them out. Since they already know you, they are now likely to give you a try.

Keep cultivating your clients in this manner until you have five good ones. Whenever you want more business, just start making the rounds as you did before.

ALWAYS MAINTAIN A LIST OF 25 PROSPECTS

One of the best ways to keep your business flourishing is to always *keep cultivating* 25 prospective clients. When one of your original 25 prospects becomes an actual client, replace it with a new prospect. Cultivate that new prospect like you did your original 25—meeting the contact(s) there, letting them get a sense of who you are, and giving them your card.

Don't give up calling on prospective clients until you have visited them at least five times. If they still have given you no business, drop them from your group of 25 prospects and replace them with someone else.

SUMMARY/CHECKLIST FOR SELLING WORD PROCESSING SERVICES

___ 1. Have business cards made.

___ 2. Compile a list of 25 companies that can use your services.

___ 3. Find out the name of the decision-maker at each of the companies.

___ 4. Make a personal visit to each of the 25 companies on your list.

___ 5. Tell each company about you and your services and leave two business cards.

___ 6. Go back to each of the companies within a few days of your first visit. Remind them who you are and leave two more business cards.

___ 7. Maintain a list of 25 *prospective* clients. As soon as one of your original group becomes a client, take that company off your prospective list and add another company that is not yet a client.

Chapter 5 DESKTOP PUBLISHING

An enterprise that will appeal to people who like to do a lot of different jobs, who can't tolerate boredom, and who have many talents is **desktop publishing.** It requires average technical and good business skills and has enormous income producing potential. It is a new concept brought about by changes in the ability to process information with personal computers and print the results on demand with laser printers. It is changing very rapidly as new products appear on the market and people discover new ways to use those products. It is one of the most promising and exciting new areas of computer technology, and one of the five best ways to make money with your computer.

This chapter will discuss, among other things, what you can use desktop publishing for, what the most promising money making areas are, and what hardware and software you'll need for your business. The marketing methods you should use are identical to those described in the previous chapter.

WHAT IS DESKTOP PUBLISHING?

What exactly is desktop publishing? It is, simply stated, the use of personal computers—with accompanying word processing, graphics, and page layout software—to produce printed materials. Today's technology allows a lone person to do the jobs that used to require typesetters, designers, graphic artists, paste-up persons, printers, and who knows how many other skilled persons. Implicit in the word publishing is the idea of preparing, then issuing printed matter for public distribution. With a computer and the appropriate software, anyone can become a publisher from his or her home, publishing reports, catalogs, newsletters, magazines, and even books.

SMALL SCALE DISTRIBUTION

The beauty of desktop publishing is that it allows specific bodies of printed material to be distributed cost effectively to smaller segments of people. In other words, with the old method of publishing, the cost of producing a book or magazine was so expensive that printed matter—except perhaps for the pamphlet or brochure—could be prepared for only a very large group of people. Now, because of the cost effectiveness of desktop publishing, a message, whether it's your own or your clients, can be produced for a small, special group with whom communication is sought. The ability to communicate through the printed word is now available to anyone who wants it, not merely those with a lot of money to invest in it.

As a desktop publisher you can do the same things with your personal computer that a traditional publishing house does with a large staff. You will combine graphics, design, page layout, and word processing into a typeset document that is camera ready for printing. Depending on the needs of your client, you may then help to market and promote the product as well. This is clearly a wonderful opportunity for multi-talented individuals who are comfortable doing many things.

The Process.

There are many steps involved in producing publication-quality material. They may include writing or editing, designing formats, layouts, and graphic presentations, and proofreading, to name a few. To be competitive, you must be able to produce attractive, professional looking pieces that work together as an appealing whole. Therefore, you will have to master the various crafts involved. However, if you do not wish to do them all yourself or if you recognize that you don't have good writing skills or an artistic bent that enables you to do an aesthetic design, there are many independent contractors that you can hire to help you out.

A desktop publishing business is more than just the production of publication-quality material, though. To establish a well-rounded and diverse business, you will want to exploit all the advantages that personal computers provide. A desktop publishing business will also incorporate writing and formatting documents, creating and adding graphics, preparing camera-ready copy for printing, doing research through on-line news and information services, keeping databases of mailing and subscription lists for yourself and for clients, maintaining demographic data for the mailing lists, and keeping all the financial records on your publishing business.

THE PUBLISHING BUSINESS

Publishing is not a new business. It is the same business that Gutenberg started 500 years ago. However, the technological improvements to an established industry will allow you to lay out pages, design graphics, and set type from your desk. It gives you the opportunity to compete with the established publishers and typesetters. A personal computer gives you the speed and flexibility to produce superb products at a lower cost.

The mega-publisher uses a team of editors, graphic artists, designers, and typesetters to produce a finished product, whether it's a book or a magazine or a brochure. These products must be edited, designed, and styled. The text must be typeset, galleys must be proofed, last minute corrections made. Desktop publishing technology reduces the team of people needed to one or two free-lancers.

Actually, the real cost saving comes by eliminating the typesetting, its associated proofreading requirements, and the subsequent corrections. The manuscript is typed only once, and the proofreading and corrections done in the computer, without having to produce a hard copy first. Errors are eliminated before the product ever leaves the computer. A laser printer produces an excellent quality end product. (If, however, actual typesetting is required, it can be done by down-loading computer text files electronically to Linotronic (CRT) typesetting machines.)

As a desktop publisher, your business operation can and may be just the same as that of a conventional publisher. You will have the opportunity to develop, produce, promote, and distribute a product. Your products, however, may be newsletters, brochures, resumes, reports, catalogs, magazines, books, company logos, or just about any other typeset, printed, or designed item that people want produced.

Desktop publishing has come into being because technology has made it possible to combine text and graphics in the computer, something that was very difficult before the development of the page layout program. Desktop publishing works in the following way: content-driven documents are text-based — word processing programs allow you to manipulate the information content of the document; design intensive documents are visual compositions — information is stored in pictorial, bit-mapped formats. You need a graphics program to manipulate or change the content of the document.

Now, page-layout programs integrate the word processing/text handling functions with the ability to handle data in a pictorial format. Because of this new technology, you can now present both types of information—text and graphics—in a single page layout program.

As an application concept, desktop publishing fills the gap between the extremes of content-driven document processing and design intensive document processing. The two are very different and used to be mutually exclusive functions. The creation of page layout computer application programs for personal computers allows text and graphics to be arranged artistically on the same page. Presently, computers can handle the full range of desktop publishing applications.

TWO BUSINESSES IN ONE

Note that there is a difference between publishing a product that you plan to market yourself and producing the design for a product as a service for your client. Producing a design for a product may entail only inputting copy into the computer, either to some specifications designated by the client or to a layout that you propose, then furnishing camera-ready copy. Publishing and marketing the product yourself means producing the entire text and design from beginning to end. It includes writing and editing the copy, planning the design, graphics, and layout.

Multi-talented desktop publishers would do this entire process themselves. The real go-getters will do all that for themselves and self-publish, usually in the form of their own newsletters and books. Newsletters can be a highly profitable, if challenging, endeavor. They are well worth doing if you have the many skills needed to pull it off, including good writing, research, marketing and other business skills.

KINDS OF PUBLISHING

In order to analyze the markets for desktop publishing more easily, it is useful to divide publishing into five different sectors: business publishing, personal publishing, academic publishing, periodical publishing, and book publishing. Each of these sectors need and use printed material that can be produced with desktop publishing. Use the brief descriptions of the needs of these five areas to generate ideas of where to go to solicit business for yourself.

- Business publishing: refers to materials that are used by companies and organizations. It includes brochures, catalogs, company reports, advertising and promotional materials, documentation for product, forms, stationery (letterhead), and internal memos.

- Personal publishing: refers to any materials for individual persons. These include anything from very personal items such as wedding and birth announcements, invitations, and greeting cards to pieces of a more serious nature such as reports and proposals. There are people and organizations who want to publish newsletters for friends, members, supporters, and others who share their interest in a given subject or field. Still others want to self-publish a book which they intend to promote and distribute themselves.Publishing a newsletter yourself, which again is an excellent method of generating income, would naturally come under the category of personal publishing.

- Academic publishing: materials produced and published for the academic field by scholars, students, and researchers. Students, graduate students in particular, want to produce attractive versions of their theses. Scholars and researchers need to print essays, reports, and research findings. This category often overlaps with other ones, particularly periodical publishing, in that academicians need to print materials in a form that can be presented to scholarly journals. Scholars and scientists also want to produce newsletters for others in the field, and sometimes even write books.

- Periodical publishing: refers to materials that are produced and distributed on a regular basis. The intervals at which they are distributed vary depending on the periodical. Most of the periodicals you would deal with — mainly newsletters, magazines, and journals — would be distributed monthly. It's possible that a newsletter or magazine might be distributed biweekly (every two weeks), bimonthly (every two months), quarterly (every three months), or even weekly. In some rare instances, as in the case of certain journals or reviews, they may be published annually. The way in which periodicals differ from other types of printed matter is that they generally have a set format in every issue and require a coherent, thematic content.

- Book publishing: refers, obviously, to publishing books. What sets book publishing apart from most other publishing is that the production time is generally longer because it involves a single, fairly long, unified piece.

HOW TO SUCCEED AS A DESKTOP PUBLISHER

Desktop publishing is a new field and, consequently, opens the door to opportunity in many ways. It is a field for entrepreneurs and, therefore, offers its rewards and successes in many ways.

The best way to succeed in desktop publishing (and just about any other entrepreneurial enterprise) is to establish a business operation in which you have several different and not necessarily related income streams. Each one of them alone may not generate enough income to support you, but the resultant combination of income from all of them will produce a nice living. As someone just starting out in desktop publishing, you will need several profit centers in your business. Some of the best areas for you to concentrate on to vary your profit centers are:

- Newsletters
- Resumes
- Data Sheets
- Proposals
- Brochures
- Direct Mail Packages
- Overhead Transparencies

This concept of having several profit centers as a safety cushion for an entrepreneurial business is much like having the perfect stool. If a stool has only one leg, it tips over very easily and you can't rest comfortably on it at all. If that one leg breaks, you will crash to the floor. If the stool has two legs, it balances more easily, but you still have concentrate on what you are doing or you will fall over. A stool with three legs is better still. But if your stool has four or five legs, you can rest easily on it, and if any one leg breaks, the remaining legs will support you easily.

When you are in business, your profit centers are like legs on this stool. It is possible that new technical developments, added competition, or swings in the public's demand for your product or service could limit the profitability of a business. If your business has several legs, you can focus your efforts on one of the more profitable areas until the time is ripe for an earnings turnaround.

NEWSLETTERS

Producing newsletters is one of the most profitable areas of desktop publishing. Both profit and nonprofit organizations, of which there are thousands, publish newsletters for their members. Small companies, CPA's, attorneys, real estate agents, stock brokers—anyone who deals with a select clientele—need good client relations, which is what newsletters provide.

For example, look at the newsletter opportunity that the intricacies of the 1986 tax law presented for small companies. They could have benefitted enormously by sending out newsletters to their clients with information on how they could help their clients with the new law: whether it was explaining it; helping them to save money; keeping them from losing money; or in other ways preparing for it. Many companies did just that. Others were just too busy, and let their competitors do it instead. The procrastinators paid the price, of course, in lost business.

Newsletters constitute the best, most cost effective client-relations vehicle available for professionals to keep their customers informed.

In addition to companies, many individuals and small groups publish newsletters aimed at specific audiences. There are an estimated 100,000 newsletters being published in the United States today in every field imaginable. Nearly all of us receives some sort of newsletter, whether it's from our alma mater, congressperson, or favorite user group. More and more newsletters for groups of people with common interests are being produced, some examples being the user group newsletters mentioned above, and economic forecast newsletters.

There is money to be made publishing a newsletter. If you have the skills, or the necessary assistance, to do a good one to a well-targeted audience and have the business skills and diligence to market it, then consider following this potentially profitable course. The best choice of a topic for your newsletter would naturally be one that you had some expertise and a good deal of interest in. The only way to interest someone else in something is to be enthusiastic about it yourself.

RESUMES

Producing resumes may possibly be one of the easiest ways to generate money as a desktop publisher. An attractive, well-produced resume is worth a lot to a person who is job hunting. By using templates to format and organize, doing resumes can be easy work. If you are also able to write resumes—to do the necessary sorting and honing to produce a good, job-generating resume—then this line will always be able to make you income while you stoke and tend your other profit centers.

DATA SHEETS

Designing specialized data sheets and forms can be very profitable. There are many companies and organizations that need custom designed forms and data sheets to meet different applications. Restaurant menus fit into this category. Menus, even at the finest restaurants, become outdated, worn out, and sometimes even contain typographical errors. You can offer every restaurant in town the opportunity to have custom designed menus typeset and printed at a copy store within hours. By having the format on disk for each customer, you can make changes within seconds. Can you think of any other data sheets that are used commercially? Price lists for all kinds of businesses is one example. Just let your imagination roam.

PROPOSALS

The lifeblood of consultants is proposal writing. Not only do proposals describe the scope of the work to be performed, they form the basis of subsequent contract negotiation. Crisp, clear, well-written, professional looking proposals get more attention from potential clients. More attention from potential clients means a greater probability of getting the job for the consultant. There are desktop publishers who specialize just in proposal writing for small one-man firms.

BROCHURES

Every product and service needs a brochure to describe its features and benefits. They help sell products and services by communicating important product information to potential buyers. They also are an important "Forget-Me-Not" for customers to take with them. Desktop publishing lowers the cost of designing and producing brochures. This cost advantage will subsequently generate a competitive business advantage for the clients of a desktop publisher. Instead of having a single brochure for each product, your clients can have many brochures for the same product, each targeted for a different market segment. Using page layout software can help you become an expert at designing brochures.

Politicians, special interest groups, consumer organizations, and other groups involved in politics constitute another group that needs to communicate with their constituents. Larger-sized brochures and pamphlets can be a great value to anyone running for office or wishing to keep their constituents informed. Between national, state, and local issues, there is a considerable need for this type of service.

DIRECT MAIL MARKETING PACKAGES

The production of materials for use in direct mail will use the comprehensive skills of the desktop publisher. These materials include sales letters, brochures, order cards, business return mailers, and novelty items. This is an area that a desktop publisher can specialize in, provided he or she has the many skills necessary to produce professional direct mail packages. In fact, if you are good at copy writing, graphics design, and business (or have an associate to assist you where necessary), it's possible to develop a comprehensive direct mail business. You can generate the sales literature for your clients, design the mailer, produce the camera- ready copy for the printer, and even maintain your customers mailing lists on your computer system. You can even do the mailing. The costs of the equipment needed to do all this is expensive, so you will have to have quite a volume of business to justify buying or leasing the equipment.

OVERHEAD TRANSPARENCIES

This is one of the areas of desktop publishing that is changing very rapidly as new products and software is developed. Anyone who wishes to put on a presentation, seminar, or workshop needs visual aids. Desktop systems now commercially available can be used to design overhead transparencies within a very short period of time. Using these tools, presentations can be changed and updated at a moment's notice. Opportunities in this area are ripe for development and evolution.

PRODUCT DOCUMENTATION

This category is very wide ranging and includes everything from producing assembly instructions for children's toys to operating instructions for computer programs. Whatever the product and its accompanying documentation happens to be, there is an ongoing business requirement to produce this kind of information quickly, easily, and professionally. Desktop publishing is an ideal way to generate these documents.

CATALOGS

It is possible to produce a specific personalized catalog on a laser writer that has the look of an expensive catalog, but is produced at much lower cost. Specific product information can be maintained in a database so that it is always current, complete, and accurate. When it is time to produce the catalog, it is only necessary to download the stored information into the page layout program and meet critical printing deadlines with inordinate control of the process.

THOUGHTS ON HARDWARE AND SOFTWARE

The most thrilling aspect of desktop publishing is the speed at which new products are being introduced to the market. Every week, there are new page layout programs, new word processors, new scanners, and new laser printers for sale. They are cheaper, faster, better, and smarter than any other product has been before in all recorded history. If you get involved in the game of watching these products develop, it becomes a major challenge just to collect the information available. You'll be swamped with details, specifications, and technicalities and you will never be able to decide which product is better.

The only hardware that you need to get started as a desktop publisher is a personal computer and a dot matrix printer. You can rent a laser printer and an image scanner whenever you need one. You can use an Apple Macintosh and LaserWriter, or you can use an IBM clone with any laser printer. At this writing, the Apple Macintosh with the LaserWriter are technically superior to any other system on the market. It has better graphics capabilities and displays each type style and type size as they will actually appear on the page. This technology is known as WYSIWYG or "What You See Is What You Get."

The IBM camp is catching up with rapidly improving graphics capabilities. There are more and better word processing programs available for the IBM systems. Improved page composition software such as Ventura Publishing and the IBM version of PageMaker provide WYSIWYG technology.

Image scanning is a fast developing technology that is being applied to desktop publishing. It was first developed to translate visual images into electronic images which could be displayed on a computer screen or printed out. You may remember the popular computer portraits and T-shirt images; those were done with scanners. Scanners are being used to produce electronic equivalent images of photographs which can be electronically pasted into a page layout by the software. Scanned images can be downloaded into a graphics design program and used as the basis of other artwork.

New technology is allowing text images to be scanned into word processing programs, edited, rewritten, and used in subsequent publications.

It is not the intent of this chapter to discuss and analyze the different systems available. Rather it is to demonstrate to you what software tools you will need. It is not necessary for you to get perfect hardware and software items. They are merely the production equipment in the business of desktop publishing. As in any business, when your production equipment wears out, or becomes obsolete, it will be replaced with newer, more cost effective tooling.

What you need to obtain at this juncture of starting your new business are the proper tools to produce the products that you want to sell to your clients. There are certain functions these tools must perform if you wish to offer a full range of services to your client.

DESKTOP PUBLISHING FUNCTION: WHAT YOU WILL NEED AND WHY

The heart of desktop publishing is the software. You will combine all these software elements to create your products electronically. You will need:

- A Word Processing Program — to handle your document processing needs.

- A Graphics Design Program — to produce art work electronically.

- A Page Layout or Composition Program — to combine text and graphics into columns and pages.

- Image Scanning Hardware and Software — optional.

- A Modem with Communications Software — optional. You would use this to download your products to a commercial typesetting machine, if you need higher resolution typesetting than you can get with a laser printer.

The desktop publisher will use these tools to design pages on the screen, arrange columns on the page, flow text into the columns, place images within the text, and choose and size the type style. You will do all of this on the monitor at your desk.

The final product that has been printed with a laser printer will vary in quality with the equipment used. The resolution of the type and images of most laser printers will be between 72 and 300 dots per inch. The resolution of commercial typesetting machines is 2400 dots per inch. That is quite significant in itself. However, you will need to examine the products of each under the close scrutiny of high magnification to determine a practical difference.

The work that you are now reading has been produced on an Apple Macintosh and typeset on a LaserWriter Plus at 300 dots per inch resolution. If you can tell the difference between this and a commercially typeset product just by looking at it, you have very good eyes, indeed.

If you ever need better resolution than is available on a laser printer, there are service centers in most metropolitan areas where you can download your work to a Linotronic 100 or Linotronic 300 typesetting machine. Most of these service centers can accept data electronically via modem.

Chapter 6 SHAREWARE DEVELOPMENT

Opportunities to earn money moonlighting as a programmer can be found in doing contract programming, developing commercial programs, writing shareware programs, and doing software translations. All of these areas require considerable proficiency as a programmer. Successful programming involves advanced technical skills. Programming requires long periods of concentration and the ability to handle details.

The business skills required will vary considerably with the opportunity. If you want to develop commercial programs, you will need considerable business experience if you expect to succeed. However, if you concentrate on developing shareware programs, you can cash in on the potential income of offering software products. Contract programming and software translations are additional opportunities for you to sell your time for extra money.

TARGETING YOUR MARKET

Who hires programmers? Most of your clients will be small business owners who need specialized software capability that is not available in commercial, off-the-shelf packaged programs. They are likely to have installed a computer system and know what software can do for them. They recognize the advantages of customized software and are willing to pay for its development. In targeting this market, look for people who:

- have specialized applications or variations of specialized applications. For example, automobile parts represent specialized problems in inventory control because of the interchangability of the parts. Even if a "Parts" program was commercially available that performed most or all of the desired functions, there may be special problems if the store manager wants to add a field to the record in the data file.

- already have a computer, but are having trouble because the application software does not exist for their system.

- want to have the security of knowing the person who developed the software and the ability to call him or her in if anything goes wrong.

CONTRACT PROGRAMMING

As a contract programmer you will be expected to develop and manage a detailed project plan. You must be able to evaluate the tasks required, the time necessary to complete them, and work them into a schedule that is acceptable to the client.

Most beginning moonlighters will underestimate the time requirements for completing a project, and then find themselves literally working by the light of the moon at the last minute to complete it. Poor quality work is the result. If it is a fixed price project, the hourly wage paid will be proportionally reduced. However, the most important quality in a contract programmer is reliability about deadlines. The habit of meeting deadlines builds your reputation faster than technical excellence. Therefore, it is of utmost importance to learn how to estimate correctly in order to make a decent income and still produce quality work.

PERFORM SOFTWARE TRANSLATIONS

There are lots of good programs that operate on just one computer. If they could operate on several computers, they would have a broader market appeal. Many times the author of the program is too busy to install it on every new computer that is introduced. You can convert the program to run on other systems and earn money in the process. You must first contact the author and the publisher to get approval.

You will need a separate language compiler, debugger, and editor for every computer system you choose to work on. For those people who are looking for a good way to obtain experience programming, this is a good way to get started. You will not need a great deal of programming skill, since the program has already been developed. Converting the program will give you a chance to study commercial level code and systems design. Just reading someone else's program to see how they did it will enhance your skills.

DEVELOPING COMMERCIAL PROGRAMS

Fortunes have been made by software authors producing the right program at the right time for the right market. Developing software is a labor-intensive industry. If you have the skill, it is a perfect opportunity for a moonlighter. You can get started for a low capital investment writing a program in your spare time.

When you have completed your program, you have two choices: team up with a marketing company who will produce, advertise, package, and distribute your software on a national scale; or sell it yourself. If you do find a software publisher to handle your program, you will receive a royalty. The remainder of the revenue will be divided between the retailer, the distributor, and the publisher.

The Market for Commercial Software.

Before you sit down and write your software package, you must decide if there is a market for it. There are thousands of programs available already. More than 34 new programs are released every day. Does the world need another word processing or spreadsheet program? Isn't the market for these items already saturated?

Some markets probably are saturated, but there are still outstanding opportunities available for new programs that fit into a specialized niche.

- Whenever a new machine, a new operating system, or a new chip is introduced, opportunities become evident. Good software programs now become obsolete. The chips are incompatible with the software running under the old operating system. Existing programs need to be converted to the new system.

- New application concepts are born. In the last five years, the concept of "integrated" software has been the buzzword. The combining of word processing, data base management, spreadsheet, graphics, and communications applications into one "integrated" package have led to fortunes for companies such as Lotus, Ashton-Tate, and Microsoft.

It would be difficult to successfully introduce another integrated package into the market today. Still, there are new opportunities developing in new classes of software that could provide the impetus for a new wave of development in still unexplored arenas. People have been talking about artificial intelligence systems for decades. It could be the time for thinking software applications. Use your imagination. If you discover the right idea, it could rocket you to success far beyond your wildest dreams.

- Micro-computer hardware is amazing. It has become more powerful in terms of memory, CPU clock speed, external storage than anyone could have imagined. The old 8-bit mini-computers with 4 K CPU's that used a teletype for a keyboard and paper tape for external storage are gone. They have been replaced by micro-computers with megabyte memories and 100 megabyte hard disks. A recent report in the *Wall Street Journal* described a project at the AT&T Bell Laboratory in New Jersey in which ways to produce chips at the molecular level have been discovered.

  Technology such as this will allow applications on mainframes to be downloaded to smaller and smaller machines. Technological innovation advances hardware. Software applications can be developed to take advantage of those advances.

Publishing Your Program Yourself.

After you have completed the task of developing the software package, you need to publish it. Unfortunately, software publishing requires a large capital investment. Advertising, writing media releases, copying the program, producing the documentation, and packaging it attractively, and placing it in retail outlets requires a very large amount of capital.

For example, if you wish to advertise your program in a major magazine such as PC World, it will cost you $12 to 18,000 for a full page advertisement. If you run it 3-6 times to get visibility, you will have invested $40 to 100,000 before selling your first copy. If you do not use full page advertisements, no one will take you seriously,

If you have not yet accumulated a large amount of capital, you will need outside financing. Venture capital is not easy to obtain. People experienced in raising venture money charge up-front fees. Unless you have had experience in raising large sums of money before, have had a successful track record producing commercial software, or have marketing talent, I would not recommend trying to publish your own software using conventional methods of distribution..

There is another way to go, though. You could start off by writing a shareware program.

WRITING SHAREWARE PROGRAMS

The major advantage of writing shareware programs is that it will not cost you any money to market your program. You do not have to spend time looking for a software publisher. All you have to do is to write a program and distribute it through user groups and electronic bulletin boards. It is not copy protected and people can copy it and use it. If they like it, they will register the program and send you a donation. Then and only then will you send them the full documentation. It's also best to offer telephone support to all registered owners, too.

Shareware publishers make money because many copies of their programs are distributed. Since so many copies are distributed, there is a good chance that someone will like it and send in their registration fee.

If people like your program and register it, your installed base will grow. Once you have a large installed base, you can make money by adding features to the program and selling the upgrades to your already satisfied customers. There are minimal marketing fees, and selling upgrades can result in substantial earnings.

ESSENTIALS OF A GOOD PROGRAM

Writing the program is the most difficult part in becoming a shareware developer. Look over the the software which is presently available on the type of computer on which you plan to do the programming. Determine the features you wish to present. Strive to incorporate originality and usefulness in your software.

Software innovation is what sells shareware. This is especially true if you want to write and distribute a game program. Unless you can develop a novel and innovative game, it will not produce much revenue. The programs which are the most in demand are productivity programs such as *PC-Write* which has grossed over $400,000 or utility programs such as *PKARC* for data compression.

Since games do not sell well, you should take advantage of the opportunity in business applications. Use this "Hip Pocket" support of shareware by business to make your venture rewarding. The reason a business person will register his program is because he needs something more from you.. It may be a fully operational version of the program, telephone support, extensive documentation, or enhancements supplied with the new versions of the software.

If you want your program to catch on, you must spend extra time to provide the following features to your software.

- The program must be SIMPLE and EASY to use. If you have included so many options and features that your users can 't get going easily, they will give up and look for another program. Remember, you are giving it away FREE on the honor system. The users of the program will not send in their money unless they are very satisfied with the results and want all the updates.

  It is different when someone purchases a commercial program for a lot of money. They will spend hours, days, and weeks trying to make it operate as it should. They are determined to get their money's worth. But it's different when someone has just acquired a shareware program *FREE*.

  The user is not very tolerant . Consequently, if your program is difficult to use, the user will not bother to find out what is wrong. He will simply trash it out of frustration and move on to something easier.

- The program must be 110% bug free. Get people you know to act as beta testers for you. Members of user's groups are good for this. They like to experiment and would help you find any defects.

- Documentation should be included with every shareware program. You can do this with an ASCII all test READMEFIRST file that the user is able to print out to obtain a hard copy.

- You must include a REGISTRATION SCREEN with your program. Usually it is the very first screen that the user sees when they start up the program. The registration screen asks the user for money. If you forget to include it, you will never hear from anyone and never collect anything for your efforts.

- It's essential that your shareware program be of high quality. If it is not, users will not register the program and you will not earn any money.

HOW TO GET DISTRIBUTION

Distribution is the key. In fact, the ability to get free distribution is the reason you went into the shareware business in the first place. How do you go about getting it?

All you need to do is to send your software to software libraries and known shareware distributors. They will do the rest. You can also place your program on Remote Bulletin Board Systems. If it is good, it will find its way around very fast.

When you start sending your software to various software libraries, you will need to include a cover letter with it. Your letter should tell them that you would like to have your program included in their shareware library. Be definite that your program is shareware and not FREEWARE.

Don't forget to include a short description of what the program does. One hundred words or so should do nicely. It is here that you will describe all the features of the program and list what computers that your program will run on. If you don't do this, the librarian will not know what to expect and your program will not be listed in their catalog. If you need help in finding the addresses of shareware libraries, send a self-addressed, stamped envelope to the author of this book and a complete list will be sent to you.

One enterprising shareware developer took a map of the United States which showed population density and stuck a pin in every metropolitan area with a 500,000 or more population base. He then called two bulletin boards in each one of those areas. Within days he was receiving orders from all over the country.

CUSTOMER RELATIONS

Always respond to your customers communications. It's an easy way to build good will and future business when someone sends you a check, you should always send them something in return. Even if it is a form thank you letter that you keep on your word processor. A brief thank you letter lets them know that you are continuing in business and will be available to help them in the future.

Another reason for responding is that your customers may or may not have the current version of the software. Some shareware programs have been available for 5 years or more. Although updates are made, there are lots of obsolete versions of the program floating around. It's good long term business to keep new registrants current.

YOUR PROGRAM

© 1989 by ASHAREWARE DEVELOPER

Please note that MYPROGRAM is a SHAREWARE PRODUCT

If you find MYPROGRAM helpful please send a check for$15.00 To (YOUR NAME). This small amount will help compensate the many months of work that went into the development of this program and will encourage the author to provide updates. If you register, you will receive all the free help you need to run this program.

Please make checks payable to:
YOUR NAME
111 YOURSTREET
YOURTOWN, USA
(800) 555-1212 if you have any questions.

THANK YOU

PRESS ANY KEY TO BEGIN

Chapter 7
BE A COMPUTER CONSULTANT

Word processing may be the very best way for someone to *begin* earning money with their computer. Computer consulting, however, offers you the opportunity to enter into a very prestigious and high paying profession. Think of word processing as the Chevrolet of computer businesses, and computer consulting as the Cadillac.

It's easy for someone with limited technical and business experience to get started as a word processor. But to succeed as a computer consultant, you need advanced business and technical skills. A word processor will earn $100 to $500 on a typical project. A computer consultant can earn from $1,000 to $15,000. Projects paying $10,000 are fairly common. Most consultants earn $65 to $75 per hour.

WHO CAN BE A CONSULTANT?

There are no restrictions on who may become a consultant. Anyone who wants to become a consultant can become one just by hanging out his shingle. With the exception of a local business license, there are no licensing requirements. Compared to most high income, high visibility professions such as those found in the medical, legal, and financial areas, there is no government red tape to contend with. You are on your own. You can go as high and as far as your ability and ambition drives you.

YOUR PRODUCT

As a computer consultant, your primary product will be a report. Sometimes it will be in writing, and sometimes it will be verbal. In any case, the report is not likely to be longer than 7 to 10 pages. You will collect a fee of $10,000 or more for something that took you four or five weeks to produce. Your product is not very tangible. Consequently, your image and credibility are very important for convincing your client that he has received his money's worth. Since typical fees for single jobs are so high, you can see why successful consultants have annual incomes of $100,000 or more.

There are, at most, five things that you will do:

1. You will study and analyze the problem. You must do this so that you can compare alternative solutions to the problem.

2. You will prepare a report summarizing the problem.

3. You will prepare a report discussing your results and findings.

4. You will make a recommendation.

5. You will implement your recommendation upon client approval. If your client does not agree with your conclusion, this step may not be performed.

These five activities may not seem very difficult, but they do require that you have the right know-how to study and analyze the problem. In addition, you must have the time to devote to this project. Finally, you need the resources to help you overcome any obstacles or roadblocks that may temporarily keep you from completing the project. The specific technical and business skills that are necessary to perform these tasks are discussed later in this lesson.

WHO SHOULD NOT BE A CONSULTANT

Everyone is not cut out to be a computer consultant. Obviously, it is a very attractive profession. In fact, I recommend that anyone with the aptitude and ability to succeed as a consultant should get started today. However, there are some factors that you should consider before embarking on a career as a consultant.

YOUR TECHNICAL EXPERIENCE

First, you must evaluate your technical experience. If you have limited experience with personal computers, it will be difficult for you to succeed as a consultant. Your clients will want to feel that you understand their problems and have the ability to solve them in a cost effective manner.

YOUR BUSINESS EXPERIENCE

Next, if you have had little business experience, you should not become a computer consultant. There are many traps and pitfalls that you can fall into. As a computer consultant, you will be expected to be an astute business person. Your clients will expect you to understand the business implications of everything you do.

FEAST OR FAMINE

Finally, the income is not consistent. Obviously, if you earn $10,000 from a single job, you may go a month or two without working or receiving any return on what you do. By starting as a moonlighter, you will not be dependent on the cash-flow from your consulting business for your survival. Still, in order to succeed over the long term, you need to be able to handle the feast or famine situation. If you are a person who needs a great deal of security, consulting may not be a suitable profession for you.

WHO USES COMPUTER CONSULTANTS?

The personal computing industry has pervaded every other industry. Every place you look you see a computer. Microcomputer chips are used in your car, your television, electronic appliances, and in your watch. This growth has contributed to prices falling to such a low level that everyone who wants a computer can afford to buy one.

Consequently, it is not just large, megabuck corporations who are placing personal computers on every desk. It is also the small businesses, retailers, wholesalers, contractors, doctors, accountants, lawyers, and independents who are having to computerize just to stay competitive. Accountants must manage and analyze large amounts of data. Lawyers are discovering the value of data base research using such electronic libraries as WESTLAW and Lexis. They do billing, handle appointments, and schedule the filing of important documents all by computer.

Any small business which in the normal course of its regular business must issue billings, maintain a mailing list, send form letters, maintain files, track inventories, monitor customer buying habits, watch credit limits, or make reservations is a prime candidate for computerization. If such businesses have already computerized, they may be able to increase productivity further by upgrading their system. In short, everybody is a candidate for computerization and can use the services of a good computer consultant. It represents a universal need that will be with us into the twenty-first century.

WHAT THE CLIENT LOOKS FOR IN A CONSULTANT

As a computer consultant, you are selling yourself. In order to get work you must convince your client that you are the right person for the job. It is necessary for you to convince him that you understand his problems and will produce a cost effective solution for them that is worth far more than the fee he pays you.

- Understanding the Client's Business. The clients that you will deal with are experts in running their businesses. Usually, they are not computer literate. They know, however, that a computer can make them money. When they hire a computer consultant, they really want someone who is both an expert in their business or industry and knows computing.

- The Ability To Communicate. The way you will convince your client that you are the right person for the job is with your knowledge of the language used in the client's business. Remember, your client will feel more comfortable with someone who not only is acquainted with computers but also knows his business intimately, than he will with a computer genius who is unacquainted with his industry.

- Common Sense Solutions. After you have made your client comfortable about your knowledge of his business, this next step is to show him that you can explain technology without resorting to jargon or computerese. Keep things simple, make your explanation easy to understand, don't be boring, and your client will buy your services.

SKILLS YOU WILL NEED

As a consultant you need a high degree of business skill both to operate your own consulting practice and to understand your clients' business problems. You need in-depth technical knowledge about what computers can and can't do. You need to be able to find the answers to questions while working on your own. Consulting is a highly skilled profession. If you do not have all the skills that you need to get started right now, there are ways of improving your skills and earning money while you learn.

TECHNICAL SKILLS

To succeed as a computer consultant, you need to know what a computer can and can't do. You need to know the differences in computers and the software that can be run on them. You need an understanding of the computer industry as a whole. You need to be current in new technological developments and in what products, peripherals, and software have been released and what products will be released soon.

It is not necessary that you be able to program, but it is helpful in understanding how software is designed.

KNOWING WHERE TO FIND THE ANSWERS

Many people think that consultants are people who already know all the answers. That simply is not true. The best consultants are the people who can say "I don't know" when they don't know the answer to a question. What they do know, however, is how to go about finding the answers. It's much more important to be able to find the correct answers than to have them in your head. By answering "I don't know, but I can find out," you've given a response that is convincing. It shows your client that you have enough confidence in your own ability to do the job that you do not have to try to bluff him. It is the mark of a true professional.

Big Red Makes a Point.

Several years ago when my Irish setter Big Red Dog was sick, I took him to the veterinarian for treatment. The vet on duty diagnosed the problem as prostatitis. It seemed like a strange illness for a one-year-old dog, but I went along with the treatment. Hormone pills perked him up for a while, but he got sick again. When I took him back the second time, I asked for the head vet. Dr. Stewart was the man in charge and he examined Red. After running a few tests, he said to me, "Mr. Mortz, I don't know what's wrong with your dog." Not very encouraging, or so I thought.

He went on to say, "It looks like prostatitis is the right diagnosis, but it doesn't make sense for a young dog to come down with it. However, there are some other possibilities. Let's run some other tests." Well, I went along with that and found out that the dog was suffering from a blood infection caused by someone trying to poison him. No wonder sex hormones were not working.

Dr. Stewart had the confidence in his own ability to say to me straight out that he didn't know what the problem was. It gave me the courage to listen to him when he wanted to do those exotic tests. There are just a very few people whom I know that will admit that they don't know something in their professional area. And every one of them is a leader in his field.

Start now to build the habit of saying you don't know something when you don't actually know it. Then go out and look it up. It's not wrong to be ignorant of something. It is wrong, however, to stay ignorant.

BUSINESS SKILLS

A consultant gives technical advice, but he or she needs to be competent in a broad range of business disciplines. In fact, consultants who have a high degree of business experience or education and a lesser degree of technical knowledge are far more likely to become successful consultants than the computer scientist specialist who has a vast knowledge of computers and little business experience or background.

BUSINESS SKILLS ARE CRITICAL

If you want your business to survive and grow, you must achieve a minimum level of competence in business. As an independent business person , you will not have anyone else to depend on. There are no staff personnel who specialize in marketing, finance, accounting, or law for you to call upon. You are on your own. Although you may have an accountant, a lawyer, and a banker, it is not always feasible to be asking them for advice on every business decision. They are professionals, too, and it may become too expensive for you to consult them regularly.

Legal

You should be familiar with basic business law. If you are not current, you should take a refresher course at your local community college. It is imperative that you understand the elements that constitute a contract. You must know how to develop a contract that is fair to both you and your client.

Accounting

You should be able to read a profit and loss statement. An understanding of cost accounting principals will help you with budgeting and making financial projections. Of course, basic accounting fundamentals go into determining your hourly billing rate.

Most accounting systems are double entry — credits and debits. Handling credits and debits is the basis for all accounting systems. If you ever get confused, just remember this story about the head partner of a prestigious CPA firm. Every morning he would walk into his office, unlock his desk, and look something up in a little black book. Over the years, his books always balanced, and the auditors never had to make adjustments to his accounts.

When he retired, he left the key to his desk to his junior partner, with the admonition, "If you ever have a problem, look in the black book in my desk drawer. The answer will be there." One day, the junior partner was having trouble with an unusually complex proceeding. He decided to follow the senior partner's advice. He went over to the desk, unlocked the drawer, and looked for the sage advice. All the pages in the book were blank except for the last one. In big capital letters were printed: THE DEBITS ARE NEXT TO THE WINDOW.

Finance

You need to be able to make cash-flow projections and handle the cash needs of your business. Where will the money come from to get your business off of the ground? How will you pay your bills while you are waiting to receive your income check from one of your clients? These are important questions and must be answered every day.

Marketing

You need clients if you are to become a successful computer consultant. How are you going to find them? How are you going to convince them that you are the right person to do their job? You must be able to analyze target markets and develop products and services that satisfy their needs and requirements. The best computer skills will go unrewarded if you can't find the means to get the word out to your potential clients. Marketing skill is essential. As an old entrepreneur once told me, the only thing that is both necessary and sufficient for the survival of a business is customers.

Administration

This is simply good management. You must organize your technical, marketing, financial, accounting, and legal skills into an entity that will work for you to build a successful consulting practice.

HOW TO GAIN THE SKILLS YOU LACK

Do not become discouraged just because some of your skills may not be as developed as you would like them to be. Furthermore, you do not have to be a combination computer genius and business tycoon in order to be a successful computer consultant. You do have to have an understanding of what is involved. Anyone with the interest, ambition, and desire can master them sufficiently to build a successful consulting practice. It is my primary concern to make you aware of what you must do; it is not my intent to discourage you or keep you from getting started.

BUILD ON WHAT YOU ALREADY KNOW

The foundation of every successful consulting practice is business skills that were gained before learning about computers. You can use your common sense business knowledge as a springboard to launch your consulting career. But in addition, take inventory of what is probably a considerable store of business knowledge—what you already know from past experience. Make a log for yourself of the answers to the following questions:

- Your present job. What skills do you use there?
- Past employment. What did you learn?
- Family business. Was anybody in your family ever in business for themselves? What can you learn from that experience?
- Volunteer organizations. Were you ever in one? How did they raise money? How were they organized? What lessons did you learn?
- Other activities? Stop and brainstorm every activity you were involved with for building blocks.

It is important that you go through this mental exercise. As I told you earlier, even if you had only a working knowledge of computers but an intimate knowledge of their business, the client will hold you in higher regard than if you are a computer genius who does not understand their business.

WHAT YOU CAN LEARN

Start talking to people you meet about the nuts and bolts of their business. Use chance encounters to find out the internal workings of different businesses. Find out why a contractor needs a different type of accounting system than a retailer. When you do receive a consulting assignment, use it to delve into as many details as possible. People will be glad to talk to you about their jobs. Get the facts first.

So many times consulting assignments are just like the dilemma of the chicken and the egg. You need to know something about the answer before you start asking questions. Business knowledge helps you ask the right questions to get the right answers.

Trade journals contain lots of information about different types of businesses. When you have an appointment with a new client in a new industry or business, go to the library for an hour or two and read some magazine articles. Be knowledgeable about the issues facing your client's industry. Remember, your familiarity with your client's business will help relax your client. He will tend to open up more about his problems and his operation. If he has to explain the workings of the industry, he will be turned off.

READING UP

Start reading software reviews for different products. One recent issue of *PCWorld* published 1,200 software reviews of different products. However, I don't advocate that you rely just on reviews to evaluate software for your client. Too often today the reviewers are competing to see who reviews a program first or how many stars they can use to rate the program. Consequently, programs tend to be feature jammed and often do more than is required by your client.

HANDS-ON EXPERIENCE

The best possible way for you to learn what a PC can and can't do is to sit down with one and use it for a week or two. There are no hardware or software requirements for you to become a consultant. You can use a dealer's demonstration hardware and software to learn, or you can purchase your own. If you do buy one, use it for managing YOUR business. Do not use your computer in your client's business. You should use his computer. If you use your computer, your client will not see you working, and will start having doubts about those high fees he is paying you. By using his computer you will need to make frequent visits to his office. He will see you hard at work on his computer and believe that those fees have been earned. This is good for client relations and will help you get follow-on work.

You must, however, know enough to operate the hardware and software. By operating a PC for a while, you can learn where your client is likely to become frustrated and give up. You can plan around these troublesome areas and keep everything running smoothly.

WHAT TO EXPECT AS A COMPUTER CONSULTANT

When you open up your consulting business, it will take some time to attract the type of clientele that you want. You are going to have an inconsistent revenue stream, and you will get lots of free advice on how to improve your marketing tactics. This is especially true when you go into a dry spell for a while.

YOUR REVENUE PATTERN

Consulting by its nature is a feast or famine business. You have to be able to ride out the rough spots and accumulate profits when times are good. When you have worked for a paycheck for most of your life, the changeability of your financial situation and your cash flow can be a very traumatic adjustment. A professional, optimistic attitude will help you through the difficult periods.

Several years ago, an acquaintance of mine, Carl, started his own consulting practice. He spent a lot of time meeting people and making written proposals. None of them were accepted. He was starving and needed money to pay the rent. I was in his office one day when the phone rang. It was from a prospect who had decided to accept a proposal submitted many months previously.

The first thing the prospect said was, "Is the price quotation for the work still valid?" At that time inflation was rampant and price increases were common. My friend, however, had financial problems and needed the work. Still, without hesitating a second, my friend said, "No, I will have to increase the price by 15 percent." As a professional, he stuck to his convictions and his price structure. What courage in the face of adversity! He got the job.

You have to keep a positive, professional, business-like attitude at all times. Concentrate on making the right business decision both for you and your client. It will help your business prosper.

One thing that Carl had done, which helped legitimatize his fee increase, was to put a time clause in the proposal he had originally submitted to the client. The time clause consisted of a specific time period for which the proposal fee was good. Because the client hadn't responded within the time designated in the proposal, Carl was justified in raising his asking price. Too many beginning consultants forget to include a time clause. Clients may respond to your proposal months after submission, demanding the original price you quoted them, even though your prices and the overall circumstances may have changed considerably.

YOUR COLLEAGUES

You will not begin consulting in a vacuum. There are a lot of people out there competing for the available work. Many of them are amateurs and give it up because they can't make any real money. Others seem to last, year in and year out. They are the professionals and you need to become one of them. Don't think of these people as your competitors—think of them as people who are going to give you the information you need to succeed.

Have you completed a survey of your competitors? Turn back to the COMPETITOR'S CHECKLIST in Chapter 3. It's a good time now to make some photocopies of it and get started checking things out.

EARNING MONEY AS A CONSULTANT

NEEDS ASSESSMENT AND SYSTEM INSTALLATION

What is a needs assessment and system installation? It is exactly what the words imply: A needs assessment consists of analyzing the computer/computing needs of a client business. If you have also been retained for system installation, you would then select and install the computing system that you feel will best take care of the needs of the company. In doing a needs assessment, you will basically have determined the following for your client: whether computerizing his office makes sound business sense. If that is found to be the case, you would then analyze which part(s) of his operation would most benefit from automating, and, finally, research what combination of hardware and software are needed.

Here is an example of a casual needs assessment I did for one businessman. I was browsing through a new computer store here in Pasadena, when I overheard a conversation between a customer and one of the salesmen. The customer was a businessman who thought he wanted to buy a computer system, but hadn't thought out why or whether he even really needed one. The salesman demonstrated the system to him, showed him all the features of the software, and still the man was hesitant. He kept talking to the salesman about potential price reductions in the next three months. "I hear that the price of the system is supposed to go down. If the price comes down another $1,000, I will buy the system," the man kept saying. When the salesman was called away for a telephone call, I started talking to the man. I asked him the sorts of questions that would give us both an idea of what his computer needs were, including, "What do you want to use it for? What will it cost? How much money will it save you? How much money will you lose by not installing the system now?"

The system in question, complete with software, was going to cost about $7,000 and save him $20,000 per year. This meant that the system would pay for itself in about four months, and generate a cost savings of $2,000 per month. I pointed out to the gentleman that he was losing $1,000 every two weeks by not owning that computer. If he bought the system in three months when the price went down, he would have lost over $6,000 by not having installed it now.

Needless to say, the man bought the system when he realized that he was losing $2,000 each and every month by not having it. (The price of the system when looked at by itself is almost always a false and misleading indicator of what should be done. What justifies a business computer is the money it will save or the income it will earn while performing a job-related task.)

Of course, the needs assessments that you will be doing will be a little more complicated than this example, but not considerably different in kind. Basically, what you're finding out in a needs assessment is what the client hopes the computer system can do for him and what jobs he needs to have done. After that, it's up to you to analyze the hows, whats, and wherefores, including if and how he can save money, streamline his operation, or whatever.

The kinds of issues you will need to find out from the client or determine for him, include:

1. What is the cost of doing business? Does the company need to control rising or excessive operating costs? Does it need to improve revenues?

2. How effective is the operation? Does the company need to improve service or product quality? Does it need to improve flexibility to meet anticipated or changed requirements?

3. How timely is the service and/or product? Does the company need to improve response to customer deadlines? Does it need to cut lead times for delivery of services and products to customers?

4. How have conditions changed in the marketplace? Does the company need to offer new services and/or products?

5. Does the company need to respond to competitive pressure to offer better, faster, broader, more complex services and/or products?

This line of inquiry will help you identify what parts of your client's business operation are valid candidates for automation. You will be looking at each part of the business operation and analyzing how it's being done and whether the computer can help the business to do it faster, easier, more accurately or to free up employees' valuable time for other tasks. One way to approach your task that may make it a little easier and will help ensure that you have touched all the bases is by working backwards from the software. By this I mean, work from your knowledge of software to determine what type of application software each of the operations fits into. Is it financial management? Accounting? Is it word processing? Is it database management, telecommunications, or graphics software? In doing this, you will see immediately if a given existing software can improve an aspect of the client's business.

Since the lion's share of your job is the survey of your client's operation, you see why it is critical to become involved in a business area that is familiar to you. You must understand all the aspects of your client's business to be able to give a competent and useful analysis of where automation can benefit him.

A word of caution here: keep a close watch to discern your client's perception of computers and their abilities. A good many business people with little or no computer experience have a somewhat warped view of what a computer can do for their company. Be careful if you get a non-computer-literate client who thinks that computerizing will completely eliminate waste, inaccuracy, and all avoidable business losses. Part of your job here, for your own sake, is to educate the client a little bit. Explain the wonderful things he can expect. All that will be outlined in your needs assessment report. Also explain that a computer system is a tool, not a wand that can magically make everything perfect. And although it is a valuable tool, it is finally only as good as the hand of the person guiding the tool. (At this juncture, you might consider explaining to him the value of good training for his people.)

NOT EVERYONE NEEDS A COMPUTER

You will find that most businesses can benefit from computerizing. Occasionally, however, you may discover that your client could indeed benefit from changes to his operation — organizational changes rather than automation. You find that the problem in your client's business lies elsewhere — illogical organization, poor data flow, poor communication channels, or inefficient individual processes. Simply cleaning up the present operation might solve the situation.

The point here is that from your findings you're not sure that the expense of a computer system could really be justified,. It is in your best interest, and your client's, to indicate the real nature of the problem in your report. Always tell your client the truth.

Recommending an expensive computer system that offered little or no improvements, or made things even more unmanageable, would not enhance your reputation. This is not to say, however, that you couldn't identify weak areas in a client's organization *and* make a system recommendation, as long as your report explains exactly what the computers can and cannot accomplish.

HOW TO DO A NEEDS ASSESSMENT

Now that you know what needs assessment and systems installation is, the natural questions are: How do you do it? How long does it take? Fortunately, the task is not as difficult as it might seem. If you need more help *How To Moonlight With Your Computer* includes an array of forms, checklists, and questionnaires that will assist you in gathering all the information you will need to do a complete needs assessment. By filling in each of the forms for each of the aspects of the business under consideration, you will have covered all the areas to be examined in a logical sequence. These forms include:

1. Business Objectives
2. Business Needs Questionnaire
3. Problem Statement
4. Solution Statement
5. Automation Questionnaire
6. Business Effects
7. Application Selection Checklist
8. Software Checklist
9. Dealer Questionnaire
10. Documentation Questionnaire
11. Software Demonstration Checklist
12. Hardware Checklist

When you have all the above information at your fingertips you are ready to analyze what the business needs of your client are and how they can be solved.

Once all the facts are in, you need to summarize them in your six-page report and recommend that your client purchase a computer system. When your client approves your recommendation, you still have to purchase the system. The actual elapsed time may be a week or two until all the equipment arrives.

Once all the equipment has arrived, you will need to install it. That might take you four or five days. Then you must help your client effect a smooth transition from the phase in which all the work is done by hand to the new automated period in which the work is done by computer.

Transition periods are difficult and stressful. The workload on the staff is doubled or tripled since they must operate their existing manual system in conjunction with the new system until all the kinks are out of it. A week is usually sufficient, depending on the scale of the job. If you have included training in your estimate, the transition period will run concurrent with the training period. Since you are performing two functions at that time, it is not correct that you charge double for time spent.

So, let's see how much time is involved in setting up a new system for a typical client. These time estimates are not hard and fast but they should help you when you are just starting out.

Needs Analysis	5 Days
Market Survey of Software and Hardware	6 Days
Report Writing	2 Days
Purchase System	2 Days
System Installation	5 Days
Transition and Training	5 Days
Total Time	25 Days

A typical job will take you 25 days. If you charge $65 per hour, your fees will be $13,000.

HARDWARE REQUIREMENTS

As a computer consultant, it is not necessary that you own a computer. You can use your clients' computer or your local dealer's demonstrator. I will reiterate that it is better from a client relations viewpoint to perform all your work at your client's location. Therefore, you never really need your own computer.

I do recommend that you choose a hardware specialty. If you service all types of computers, it's too easy to lose the focus that is necessary for you to establish your expertise and credibility in your client's eyes. Start out by concentrating on computer systems, both hardware that you are familiar with. You must keep one important fact in mind, however: your experience must fill a need if you are to be successful.

Don't feel locked into one system. If you have worked with Commodore, you will have a different type of clientele than if you have worked with Macintosh or IBM PC's. Do not turn down a job just because you have not worked on that system before. If you feel that you are competent and have the ability to find the answers, take the job and rely on your competence and abilities.

MARKETING YOURSELF AND YOUR CONSULTING BUSINESS

The credentials that you will use to convince your client that you are right for the job are different than you are used to providing. Remember, your clients will hire you for your ability to solve problems. The best way to demonstrate that ability is to show them how you have solved similar problems for somebody else. You will use a job portfolio to do that. A job portfolio is something that you will use and expand as you become more experienced as a consultant. However, if you have not yet obtained your first client, there will be little you can place inside it. You'll learn how to start your portfolio later in this section.

YOUR JOB PORTFOLIO

Your job portfolio is the basic package of promotional materials that you will use to establish your expertise in the eyes of your potential clients. At some point, your client will want to know what you have done. You will hand your portfolio to your client and let him page through it. It will speak for you.

What It Will Say

Your job portfolio will define you. It will tell your client who you are, what you are doing, how you are doing it, and how you have solved problems before. What's in it? Photographs of systems you have installed, letters of recommendation, articles that you have written, articles that have been written about you, and anything else that you think will demonstrate your ability.

When you show it to your client, he probably won't read it very closely at all. Most likely he will just scan it and look at the pictures. In fact, the pictures that you have taken of computer systems you have installed will speak louder than anything else you can say. Some consultants recommend that you be in the picture shaking hands with the president of the company. A picture is worth a thousand words. That shows someone else telling the world how great a job you did.

Your First Portfolio Entry

The job portfolio is very powerful. Just one picture and one letter of recommendation is enough to persuade your clients that you are the right guy. What's more, it's not hard to get one started. Let me tell you how easy it can be.

The other night, I was meeting with some friends at Joe's home. During the meeting Joe announced that he had just purchased a new Radio Shack Tandy 1000 SX. He wanted to get started using it, but was afraid of it. One of my colleagues, David, who is a professional computer consultant, stayed after the meeting to coach him. When he finished, I snapped a photograph of David shaking hands with Joe in front of this $4,000 system. David plans to put the picture in his portfolio and caption it "Home Office Installation for Mr. Joseph X."

You can do the same thing. Perhaps you can do an installation for a relative or a friend, and document that with a photograph. Even if someone else has made the installation or if you've just assisted in doing it, take a picture of it anyway. That picture of someone else saying how good you are will be the first entry in your portfolio until you can begin filling it with increasingly impressive material.

PORTFOLIO CONTENTS

You can put just about anything in your portfolio that will help you to promote your business. Letters of recommendation, testimonials, photographs, articles you have written, publicity (articles written about you), and press releases. Even if the press release was not printed, you can put it in your portfolio.

Letters of Recommendation

Every time you have a consulting assignment, you must get a letter of recommendation from your client. It is very important. However, if you wait for him to suggest it, you will wait a long time, no matter how hard you have worked or how great a job you have done. He is just too busy with his own business to think of it. Ask him for it.

When you ask for a letter of recommendation, 99 times out of 100 the client will say, "Sure, I'll be glad to write a letter for you." Now you both know that either he will not have time to do it, or it will be placed in his basket of good intention. But as we know, things in good intentions baskets simply don't get done. So, in order to help your client out and to get the letter so you have it for your portfolio, proceed as follows. Say to him, "I can write it for you." Then do just that.

Press Releases

Almost all newspapers are interested in local news or events. Send out press releases to your local papers describing what you are doing. Speak at a local user's group, at a school, or at the library. Have pictures taken at the event, and send them in to your paper. When the article and/or the photograph about the event are published, you have another valuable item for your job portfolio.

Putting It Together

Assemble your job portfolio in a 3-ring binder. Make the binder an expensive looking one, with a leather cover and your name embossed in gold on the cover. Gather all the various items you have generated and place them in plastic sleeves that you buy at office supply stores to protect the pieces. Then insert the items in your binder in chronological order.

You don't want to leave your portfolio with your client — just show it to him or her. Portfolios have been lost and misplaced. If you lose it, the material contained in it is often irreplaceable. By using an expensive leather binder your client will know it is not a hand-out or or something you want to leave behind. Most clients will not expect you to leave it. The expensive look of your portfolio will help any client to understand why you are reluctant to leave it.

References

After looking at your portfolio, a client may want to call the people who have given you letters of recommendation. Be prepared for such a request by having a separate sheet prepared with the names of former clients, culled from your portfolio, who are willing to accept his call (and who are likely to give you the best recommendations).

In brief, you must perform a market survey to identify the needs and requirements of the people you are going to be selling your services to. If you have done computer consulting in the past, you have a list of former clients that you can call or take out to lunch. By talking to them and LISTENING, you can determine what their needs are. If you are just starting out, you must perform this LISTENING function and still promote your service.

PERSONAL PROMOTION

Computer consulting is a service and must be sold as a service. That means meeting people in person and talking to them. You must listen to find out what their needs are. You must ask them for referrals, and you must get them to help you develop your job portfolio.

The American Business Lunch

All important business is done at lunch. If you wish to be a professional consultant, you must act like a professional. That means that you must call your prospective client on the telephone and invite him or her out to lunch.

Now, when you invite a prospect to lunch, it is understood that YOU are going to pay. It is important that you do buy lunch, because you are really buying something that is much more valuable than just a meal. You are buying an hour or two of their time.

By taking them out to lunch, you gain some very important advantages. They are no longer in their office surrounded by the accoutrements of power. They are not sitting behind a desk. They are not subject to telephone calls and interruptions. How much is that worth to you? Far, far more than the cost of the lunch. The average industrial sales call costs approximately $275. The average business lunch costs $25 to $30.

If you take a different client to lunch every day for a month, you will spend $538 to $645. You will have talked to 22 people and have most likely landed a contract. There are not many businesses that you can get started for $500. Consulting is one of them.

Cold Calling

Who do you take to lunch? Ideally, you should take the person who has the money to buy your services and the power to authorize the purchase. When you are consulting for small businesses, it is the owner who has that power. Just start calling businesses that you have targeted as good candidates for computerization and invite the owner out to lunch. Now who can refuse a free lunch? For now, your best option is to call a prospective client and introduce yourself. Be brief. The whole conversation should take less than 30 to 45 seconds.

Say, "I am (your name). I'm a computer consultant and I would like to tell you over lunch sometime about what I may be able to do for you company." Now there are not many people who are going to refuse a free lunch. Those people who do probably are not good prospects anyway. You did some preliminary qualifying when you used the words "computer consultant." You also offered a promise of a reward—a free lunch—if they will listen to you for an hour or so. Most people will say, "Sure." Then the most important thing you can say is, "Let's do it tomorrow."

At your first meeting, drop by the person's office and pick him up. That way you will not be kept waiting at the restaurant or forgotten all together. In fact, you should confirm the appointment on the morning before the lunch and remind the person you will be picking him up. Go to a nice businessman's restaurant. It should be moderately priced; not too expensive, but not a cheap greasy spoon either.

Listening for Needs

While you are at the restaurant, get the prospect to talk about himself and his problems. Be a good listener. Use phrases like "Tell me more," "Go on," "That's interesting," and "I understand." By letting the client talk, you will accomplish two things. First, by spending all that time talking about himself, he will have established a social obligation. Since you have listened to him, he will be obligated to listen to you. Second, you will have learned some of the details of his business. You can use that information to show him that you understand his needs and can solve his problems.

Eventually, when the lunch winds down, he will realize that he has been doing all the talking. At that point he will ask you to tell him about what it is that you do. Just say you are a computer consultant. To say anymore will just confuse him. If he wants to know more, he will ask you specific questions.

Showing Your Job Portfolio

When he asks you to tell him about yourself and what you do, you'll know that the time is ripe to show him your job portfolio. You'll have brought it with you to the restaurant and have it handy. It will not need any explanation. Let it speak for you. Let him leaf through it, looking at the pictures or asking who various people are. When he is ready to take the bait, he will ask you what you can do for him. He is hooked and wants a proposal.

The Proposal

Proposals are necessary parts of a consulting practice. First, they define what work you will perform, when you will do it, and how you will get paid. Second, if accepted by your client, they can become binding contracts. So be careful what you put in them.

It's not necessary for you to compose a 300-page magnum opus; neither is it professional to scribble a few ideas on the back of a napkin. You are expected to produce a tidy two-page proposal. If you can keep it on one page, so much the better. It's best not to go over three pages. Most of it will consist of boiler plate, or standard, paragraphs that you should use in every proposal.

The meat of the proposal will be one or two paragraphs which state what you will do. Notice I said state *what* you will do. It is not necessary to tell the client HOW you will do it; just tell him WHAT. If you say too much at this stage, your client may be overwhelmed and decide not to proceed. It's also conceivable that your "how to" advice will give him enough information to proceed on his own.

The completed proposal must contain three vital elements:

1. It must convey to the client that you understand his problem and have the ability to solve it.

2. It should show him how he will benefit upon completion of the job.

3. A time limit for acceptance of the proposal.

In their haste to get their first client, many beginning consultants forget to include the time limit. Think back to the story I told earlier in this lesson. The inclusion of the time limit gave my friend Carl the opportunity to raise his price.

USING DEALERS

Having good relationships with computer dealers is a good way to direct business your way. Dealers usually do not have the time or expertise to help people find the right computer system. Yet, if they know you are available and reliable, you can be of great service to them by finding the right software and hardware for your client. You then recommend that your client purchase it from the dealer. It's a WIN/WIN situation for everyone.

SEMINARS

Speaking appearances at seminars, trade shows, and conferences is an excellent way to attract potential clients. Your billing on the roster of a seminar makes you an expert. This billing will allow you to establish a Teacher-Student relationship between you and your client. People will approach you after your presentation to ask you questions about their computer problems, which you should answer graciously. Their approaching now gives you a great opportunity to qualify them as potential clients.

PRICING YOUR SERVICE

Setting the price for your service is one of the most critical aspects of establishing your consulting business. This means more than just determining your hourly billing rate, although that is obviously an important task. Pricing your service also entails pricing larger jobs and fixed price jobs, handling clients who balk at the price, making house calls, taking travel time into consideration.

DETERMINING YOUR FEE

In order to quote the price, there are only two things you need to know:

- the number of hours it will take you to complete the job
- your hourly billing rate.

Your Billing Rate

There are many techniques that you can use to set your billing rate. The simplest by far to to call other consultants and find out what they are charging. Then you can charge the same thing. By following that procedure, you will be able to come up with an hourly rate that is both competitive and fair.

Estimating The Time

I wish I could give you a sure-fire method of making estimates of the time requirements for completing a job. Estimating is difficult, and you will need to learn through experience how much time it will take for you to perform different tasks. All I can say, is that most estimates are low.

The scenario usually goes something like this: I know I tend to make low estimates but I am trying to get the work and I hope a low price will help convince my client to hire me. Consequently, I pray that everything proceeds as planned and that I have made a lean and mean assessment of the client's problem.

Unfortunately, one of the problems is that the client doesn't always tell you the whole story about his business at that initial meeting. When you begin the project, there will be surprises that were not discussed. It is not that the client was trying to hide anything, he simply did not think about it at the time, or he did not realize how much of an effect it would have.

To compensate for this tendency to produce low estimates, I usually include a contingency or safety factor in my estimate. How much should it be? If you are doing contract programming, the client will usually want changes. Every change causes much more work than is first apparent. Programming requires a safety factor of 100 to 200 percent of the initial estimate. If you are doing a needs assessment and system installation, a 20 percent safety factor should be sufficient.

NEGOTIATING THE PRICE

If your estimate is more than your client wants to pay, it's okay to negotiate the price. However, I recommend that you NEVER negotiate your billing rate. You must, instead, negotiate the scope of the job. Cut down what you will do—the little extra tasks that put special bells and whistles on the project. This will reduce the price of the job to your client. If you start cutting your hourly rate, you will look like an amateur. It simply is not professional to cut your rate.

IF YOU UNDERESTIMATE THE JOB

What do you do if you underestimate the job? You find out that the job is really going to take longer than you expected. You just did not understand the situation sufficiently to make a good estimate. It's simple. You eat it. You are in business to make a profit, but you also have a moral and ethical obligation to your client. Get started now establishing a reputation as a professional who brings his jobs in on time and within budget.

IF YOU OVERESTIMATE THE JOB

Do not think that overestimating a job will put extra money in your pocket. Don't try to convince yourself that this overage will help compensate you for the times that you underestimated jobs and had to work on your own time to complete them within budget. Now is the time to build your reputation further. You charge your client for the actual time spent. Tell your client that the job went better than expected and that you will be charging less money than the original projection.

You just did something no one else does. You acted in the best interest of your client. Just wait until he tells his friends. Just wait until he writes "his" letter of recommendation telling the world how much money you saved him. This is the stuff that great client relations are made from.

FLAT RATES

There will be times that you will be approached by private individuals who can't afford to pay as much money as others. Under those conditions, you should have flat rates for those types of jobs. If it takes more time, so be it. You must look at enhancing your reputation as a person who is always willing to help other people.

HOUSE CALLS

There will be times when your client calls you for post-installation advice. If you can answer his question in five minutes or so, go ahead and do it without charging him. If it is a problem that you should have handled, go back and fix it. Warranty work is a cost of doing business. Use it to promote your relationship with that client. Tell him no charge. Take him out to lunch, listen to his problems. Maybe it's time to upgrade his system. Perhaps he has thought of another friend or two who could use your services. Look at this as an opportunity, not a crisis.

However, if his secretary/girl-Friday has just quit, and he wants you to train her replacement, that is a new project. You must charge for on-going service such as this. Speak up and tell your client, nicely, that this is additional work and that you will be charging for it.

THE PRICE-SENSITIVE CLIENT

Whenever you encounter a client who balks at your rates, the natural tendency is to educate the client on how your rate is determined and show him why it is cheaper to hire you than to hire someone else. Most of the time, you will be well advised not to try to explain why you charge what you do. A better strategy is to try to find out why he thinks you are expensive. Ask him, "Expensive compared to what?" Price may not be his real concern.

If it is, he is not the right client for you to be dealing with. His objection on price will show you that you are going to to have further troubles down the road. Use it as a warning signal that you may have trouble collecting your fee when you have finished the job. There are a lot of things that can happen. I recommend that you do not argue with him about price, or try to educate him about how your fees are determined. The best approach in the long run is to part amicably and look for another client.

TERMS OF PAYMENT

Getting paid is the best part of any job. As a consultant you will find out that there are potential clients out there who want you to work for them, but they don't want to pay you. So, before you begin work, you have to include those terms in your proposal and in any subsequent contracts.

FIXED PRICE

If you are working on a fixed price project, you must always ask for a deposit before you begin work. It's customary, so don't let anybody talk you out of getting it. For small jobs, ask for a 50 percent deposit and 50 percent upon completing the job. For larger jobs, you may start for 30 percent down, another 30 percent at the halfway point, and the remaining 40 percent when you have completed the project.

PROGRESS PAYMENTS

By accepting half down and the rest upon completion for jobs of longer duration than two months, you could wind up waiting a long time for your money. When you land a job that will take more than two months to complete, you must provide for periodic payment in your proposal. The intervals can be based on time, or they can be based on progress. Both methods are equivalent.

I like to be paid as often as possible. I would ask my clients for payment at the end of every day, if I thought they would agree to it. However, most clients are reasonable and will agree to pay you every week. That is the longest interval you should go. If you bill monthly, you could end up waiting three or four months for your money. If there should be some problem in getting your money, you become aware of it quickly.

Chapter 8
FOUR TRAPS TO AVOID

Although I believe that you can earn money with your computer doing just about anything that interests you, there are some ways that are more difficult than others. If you have the desire and the business acumen, and the ability to persevere, you will be successful, no matter how you choose to start. The purpose of this section, however, is to warn you about some of the traps or pitfalls you might fall into if you are not forewarned.

WHY THESE WAYS SHOULD BE AVOIDED

There are, obviously, people who are presently earning money performing accounting and bookkeeping services, operating as an information broker, and trying to become a software locator. At this point, though, each of these ways present monumental obstacles, for varying reasons, that must be overcome before a significant amount of money can be earned doing them. Therefore, if you are interested in pursuing any of these businesses, you must consider very carefully how you will enter these fields and how you will deal with the obstacles.

The obstacles vary considerably. For example, the field may require specialized knowledge. In the case of accounting and bookkeeping services, accounting knowledge will, naturally, be necessary. In addition, accounting knowledge is subject to accreditation. Unless you are a CPA or an established public accountant, it may be difficult to prove your abilities to your client. Information brokerage requires familiarity with data bases and the ability to search them quickly and easily. It is a library science which must be learned in due course. If you are not familiar with data base research, you may pay a high price to learn.

Next, there are marketing difficulties to overcome. There are no easy ways to sell these services. The markets tend to be fragmented with small numbers of potential clients. The cost of finding a client may become too high to return a profit on these activities.

Finally, there may be established players in these fields. Their names are so well known to the public that they monopolize most of the business. It's good to have competitors, but sometimes the competition can become so fierce it will ruin any new entrant into the game. Your survey of the competition can do a lot to tell you what you will be up against.

SOFTWARE LOCATOR

Becoming a software locator on paper seems like a great growth opportunity. What this business entails is compiling listings of what software is available for each type of computer. These listings are entered into a data base so that you can cross reference several categories. You then obtain clients who are looking for specific types of software. By interrogating the data base, you will be able to find a list of available software to fit their specific requirements.

This is better than a software directory, since directories become obsolete very fast. An on-line directory like this is can be updated every week, or every day, if need be.

Sounds like a very useful tool that a lot of people would be interested in using, doesn't it? There's only one problem: I haven't been able to find anyone doing it successfully. Obviously, other people also think it's a great idea for a profession. The American Association of Entrepreneurs even published a start-up manual for this business. I questioned them further, but I have not received an answer on anyone doing it. They told me to check the yellow pages. You know what checking the yellow pages will tell you. They are all out of business. Paul and Sarah Edwards, columnists for *Home Office Computing* magazine told me that they had a call from a man who claimed to earn $100,000 per year doing it, but that is all they know about it.

If any of you know of someone doing this successfully, please write to me at the American Institute Of Computer Technology and tell me who they are.

INFORMATION BROKER

Becoming an information broker is another idea that looks appealing, but should be avoided for the time being. There are people, to be sure, who are actively involved in performing this service. There are people who highly recommend this line of work as a home business. However, unless you know what you are getting into by becoming an information broker, I recommend you set it aside as an option for the time being.

The concept of the business is quite simple. You seek out published sources of information/data that suites your client's purposes. You do this by interrogating certain public data bases by modem to find the information either on-line, or a bibliographic reference to it in printed form. Once you gather the data, you will run it through your word processor to organize it and make it easier to understand. Finally, you will submit the report to your client.

PROBLEMATIC ASPECTS

There are three very important items that you need to consider before jumping into this business. First, you need to have a lot of specialized knowledge. It is a library science and you need to know how information is stored in data bases. Second, until you learn how information is organized on different public data bases, you could run up considerable connect charges while you are exploring the data base. Receiving a bill for $400 dollars for computer time on a project for which you can charge only $250 will not be pleasant.

Finally, there are considerable marketing difficulties to be overcome. The people who use information brokers – your potential clients – are hard to find. They are scattered throughout many different industries located in different parts of the country. Smaller advertising firms and consulting companies working of special projects and need information they can resell to their clients. The fragmented nature of this industry will make marketing very difficult because these small companies may only use your service once every two years.

HOW TO DO IT IF YOU'RE GOING TO TRY IT

Once you have been in business for a while, it is possible that you will run across people who need specialized research and are willing to pay for it. Over a period of time, you can develop a list of clients that will justify concentrating on this type of business.

Wait until you have the clients to get started as an information broker. This will keep your marketing expenses under control. When you have found someone who needs research services, you can then act as a broker, and subcontract the actual data base research to a professional—someone who is already doing it and knows how to access the information cost effectively. Your net profit will be diminished, but you can learn from this seasoned research worker. They can tell you things about what they did that will help you at a later time.

ACCOUNTING SERVICES

It may seem as though offering bookkeeping or tax preparation services would be a good way for you to earn money with your computer. Several years ago, it was. Today there is just too much competition in the field.

BOOKKEEPING SERVICES

You would expect it to be easy to use a personal computer to perform bookkeeping services for small businesses. However, CPA firms are now offering computerized bookkeeping at cost in order to more effectively market their other services. The CPA only needs to input the information. On an incremental basis, it costs him very little. He already has the computer and the data entry clerk. Every month when the profit and loss statements are prepared, the CPA will know how his clients are doing. He is right on the scene to sell them the high priced CPA services. How are you going to compete with a CPA?

TAX PREPARATION

Every year lots of people earn extra money preparing income tax returns for other people. However, most of these people work for companies such as H & R Block. If you want to become a computerized tax preparer, expect some tough sledding.

Even if you have a clientele and use a computerized tax preparation program, the tax code is revised and the tax forms changed every year. You are dependent on the software developer to send you the updated forms in a timely manner. Some of them do; some of them don't; some of them are out of business.

Chapter 9
EPILOG

Congratulations! By reading *Make Money Moonlighting* you have successfully completed the first step of a great life-long adventure. In fact, your own business can be one of the most rewarding experiences of your life. I ask only this – get started today!

Getting started today is very important because the experience you gain from operating your own business will make you aware of new opportunities which open up to you. By starting your first venture you will place yourself in a position to start additional, more profitable ventures which appear along the way. The act of getting in business draws opportunity to you like a magnet. You gain new contacts, gather information you never knew existed, and meet suppliers of essential goods and services. This energy generated by all this activity is what opens the door of opportunity.

Make Money Moonlighting has given you the tools to become successful by using your competition. You can profit from the ideas that are working and avoid the traps and pitfalls that deplete your capital, your energy and your enthusiasm. If you let them, your competitors will tell you how to get a competitive advantage. Have you copied the COMPETITOR'S CHECKLIST and started checking things out?

Spend some time investigating how other people are profiting. Information takes time and effort to collect. It is not a FREE commodity; it has value. That is why you must value it and do everything necessary to obtain it. I have shown you how to do it, but only you can do it.

You've also had an opportunity to examine the very best way to earn money with your computer — consulting. You've had an opportunity to discover the very easiest way to earn money with your computer — word processing. And you've seen why some ways — no matter how appealing they may appear — should be avoided.

Of the the four best ways presented in this book, one way, — word processing — requires a low level of technical skills and a low level of business skills. A second way — desktop publishing — requires a low level of technical skill but a high level of business skill. A third way — shareware development requires a high level of technical skill, but a low level of business skill. The fourth way — computer consulting requires a high level of business skill and a high level of technical skill. If you wish to sell a product, you should consider desktop publishing or shareware development. If you wish to sell a service, you can consider word processing or consulting.

Obviously, these are not all the ways to earn money with your computer. There are 102 ways that we know about. By starting with the easiest, and advancing to the best while avoiding the worst, you have the important bases covered. There's something here for everybody.

Do not hesitate to utilize any of the marketing or business ideas presented in the text to promote any business you may be involved in. The marketing ideas are sound and are truly representative of the best marketing concepts that I can show you. Just because you read about the JOB PORTFOLIO in

Chapter 7 BE A COMPUTER CONSULTANT, it doesn't mean that you can't use it to promote your desktop publishing business. *YOU CAN !*

If you need more business development information, or want more insight into those other ways to earn money, I recommend that you obtain a copy of *How To Moonlight With Your Computer.* For your convenience, an order coupon is included at the end of this book. It is the advanced text and addresses more issues than can be presently covered.

Finally, if you have any questions on the material, or would like information on more of our books and seminars, you can write me and I will do my best to answer your question or put you in touch with someone who can. Your comments or suggestions that will make the next edition of this volume better or more insightful, would be appreciated.

John R. Mortz
Pasadena, California
July 1989

TAKE CONTROL OF YOUR LIFE

- **Use *How To Moonlight With Your Computer*** to help you obtain your own profitable business.
- Profit from the promotional methods of 73 successful entrepreneurs – not dark, deep secrets, but common-sense techniques which anyone can do.
- Reap the fruit of your effort – it's by having your own business that allows you to become financially independent.
- Live a better and more enjoyable life
- Earn more money

How To Moonlight With Your Computer will show you how to make something happen. It's not a compilation of get rich quick schemes which don't work or can't be duplicated by anyone. It is an advanced, pragmatic business-development manual aimed at helping you attain the success you deserve. But you will have to work at it.

How To Order

Simply Call us on the ***HOTLINE – 24 Hours A Day*** or fill out the coupon on the next page and mail it to us. You can send your check or use MasterCard or Visa. Your book will be shipped the same day. The faster you order , the sooner you'll start earning extra money. So mail in the coupon, or call, today!

24 HOUR HOTLINE: **(818) 793-8429**

««« THE MOST FOR YOUR MONEY »»»

How To Moonlight With Your Computer is a goldmine of information. Here's what you get:

- Large 8-1/2" x 11" format lets you open the text flat and photocopy full size forms, checklists, and worksheets.
- 336 pages of unrelenting practical advice
- 32 Forms, checklists, & worksheets save you time
- This book is COMPLETE. Here's a partial list of the subjects covered:
  - The 11 Best Businesses For the 1990's
  - How To Determine Which Business Is Best
  - The Success Formula
  - Successful Moonlighting Step-By-Step
  - Seventy Three Examples of Other People Earning Money With Their Computers.
  - Your Start-up Plan
  - How To Find Customers
  - Making Sure Your Customers Buy
  - Advertising – When To Use It and When Not To Use it
  - How To Set Your Fee
  - Your Home Office
  - Software is Smart – It Makes You Money
  - The Power Lunch
  - How To Be Perceived As "The Expert'
  - How To Use Word-Of-Mouth Promotion

YOU RISK NOTHING! Get your copy of ***How To Moonlight With Your Computer*** and use it for up to thirty days. Prove to yourself that it's worth more – far more – that what you've paid for it. If you're still not 100% satisfied for any reason whatsoever, return it to us and your money will be refunded...NO QUESTIONS ASKED. Although we have sold thousands of copies of ***How To Moonlight With Your Computer,*** only 11 people have ever returned a copy for a refund.. No matter how hard you try, you can't please everyone.

The cost of ***How To Moonlight With Your Computer*** is only $39.95 plus $5.00 shipping and handling. California residents add $2.60 sales Tax. This is a remarkably low sum when you make one simple comparison – the price of the manual versus the money you can make by using it.

- -

The American Institute Of Computer Technology
30 N. Raymond Ave., Suite 714
Box 2615
Pasadena, CA 91102-2615

_____**YES,** Please send ***How To Moonlight With Your Computer.*** I understand that I have thirty days to examine the material. If I am not 100% pleased, I will return the manual for a full refund. I have enclosed my Check _____, Cash _____, Money Order _____, Visa_____, MasterCard _____ for $39.95 plus $5.00 shipping and handling. California Residents add $2.60 sales tax.

_____**MAYBE,** I am not ready to start moonlighting with my computer. But I would like to hear from you when you have the facts on other ways to earn money with my computer. Keep me in mind.

NO, I am not interested and here's why: ____________________
____
____

Amount Enclosed : $____________________

Card Number ______________________________

Expiration Date______________

Telephone (______) - ________________

Signature ______________________________

Name ______________________________

Address ______________________________

City ________________State______ ZIP ________

- -